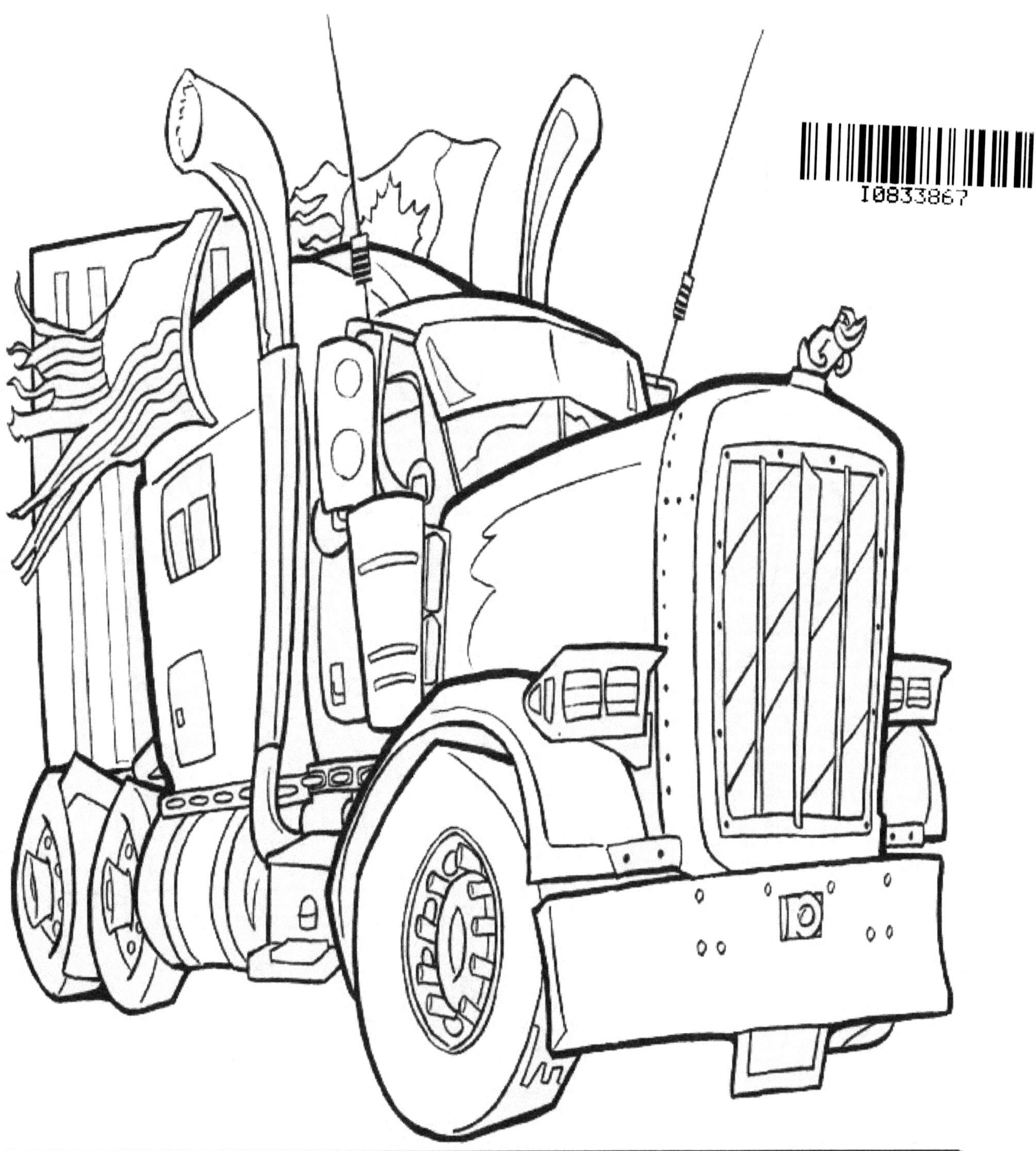

I0833867

- There are Almost 2 Million Semi-Trucks in the USA!
- A Semi-Trucks engine can last for as much as a MILLION miles!

Hope You Brought Snacks

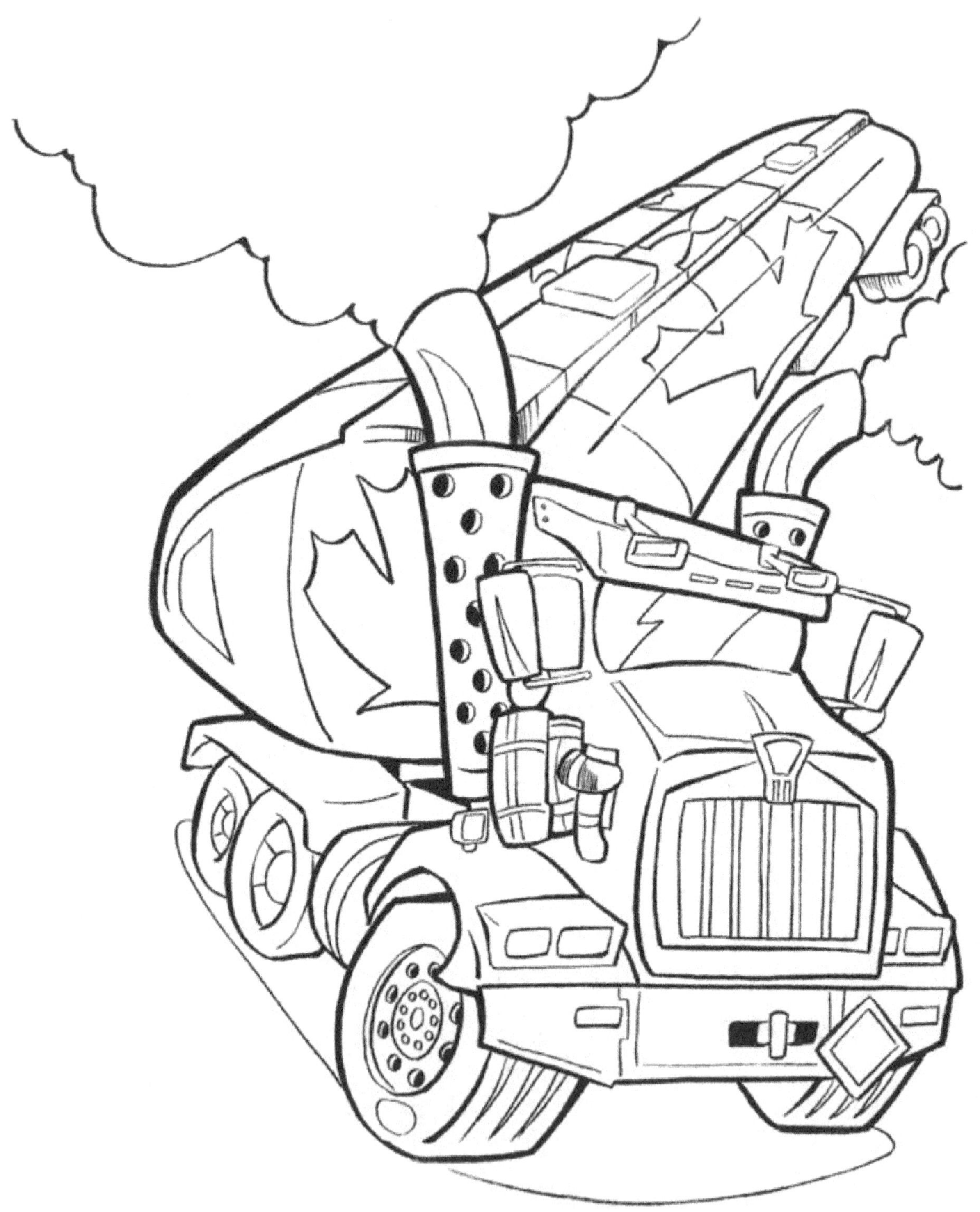

- **Diesels can Travel 30% More per Gallon of Fuel vs Gasoline -Every Mile Counts!**
- **Fuel Tankers use Specialized Membraned Tanks & Multi-Layer Vacuum Insulation!**

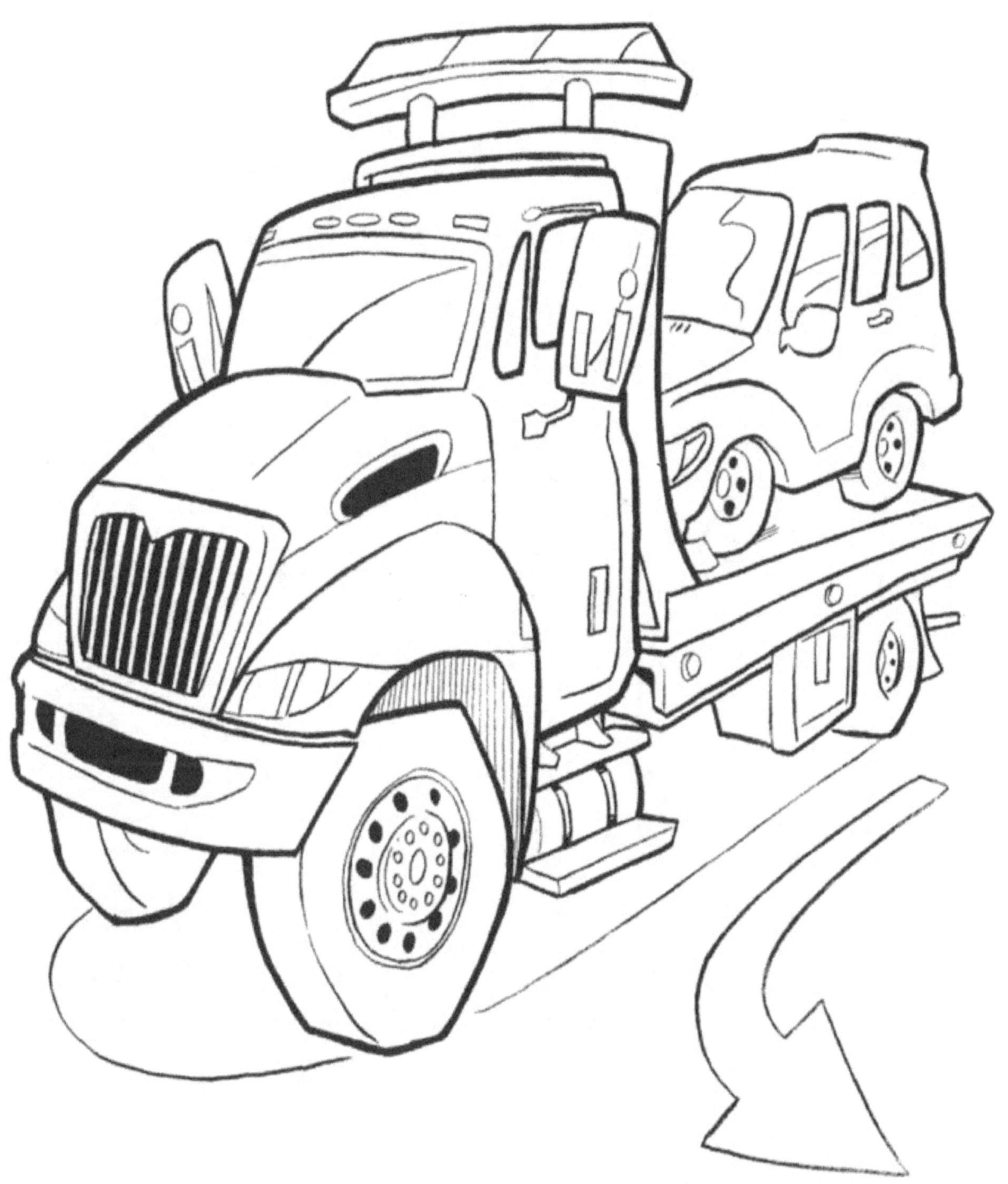

- The First Truck "Cabs" were Built to Haul Cars Man! Cars are lazy
- As of 2019, There were Around 4500 Car Hauling Companies in the U.S.!

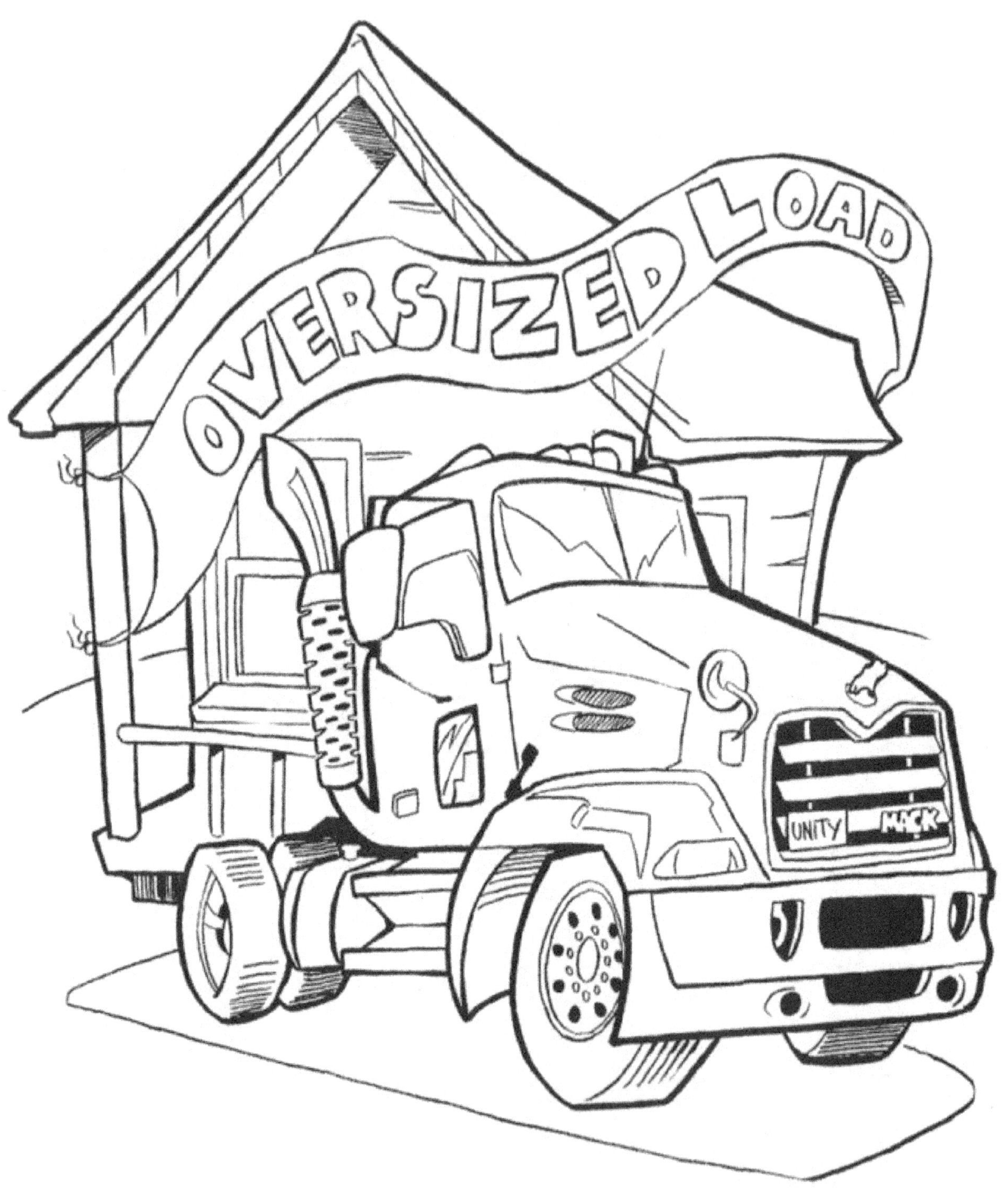

- In the United Kingdom, Tractor - Trailers are Known as "Articulated Lorries"
- The Average Tractor - Trailor can Haul weight Equal to 450 People! Heavy, Man

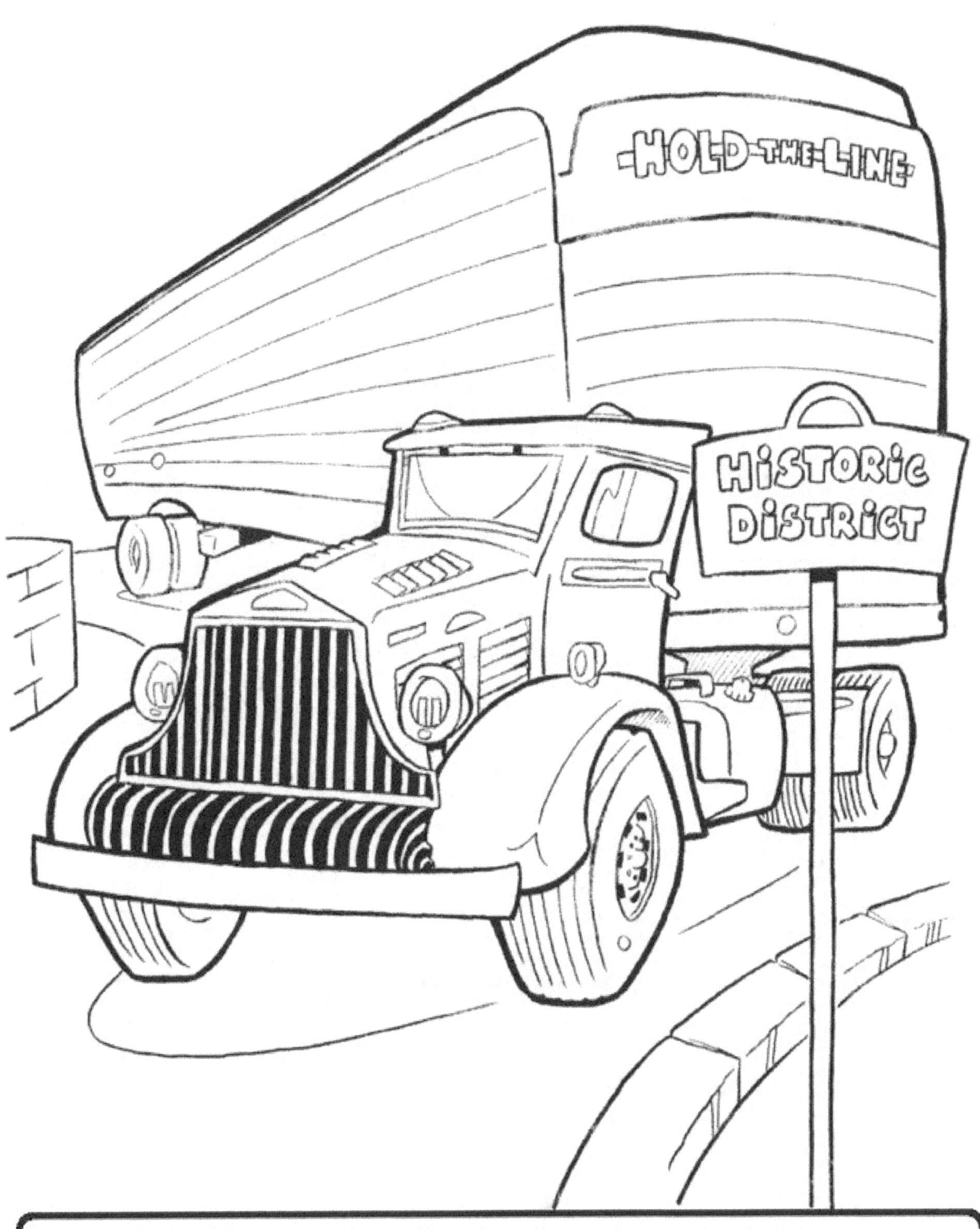

• The Term "Semi" Refers to a trailor with Wheels on One End

• The First Semi-Truck was Invented in 1898 (Alexander Winton)

The Car Radio? 1926 Hope you Like to sing!

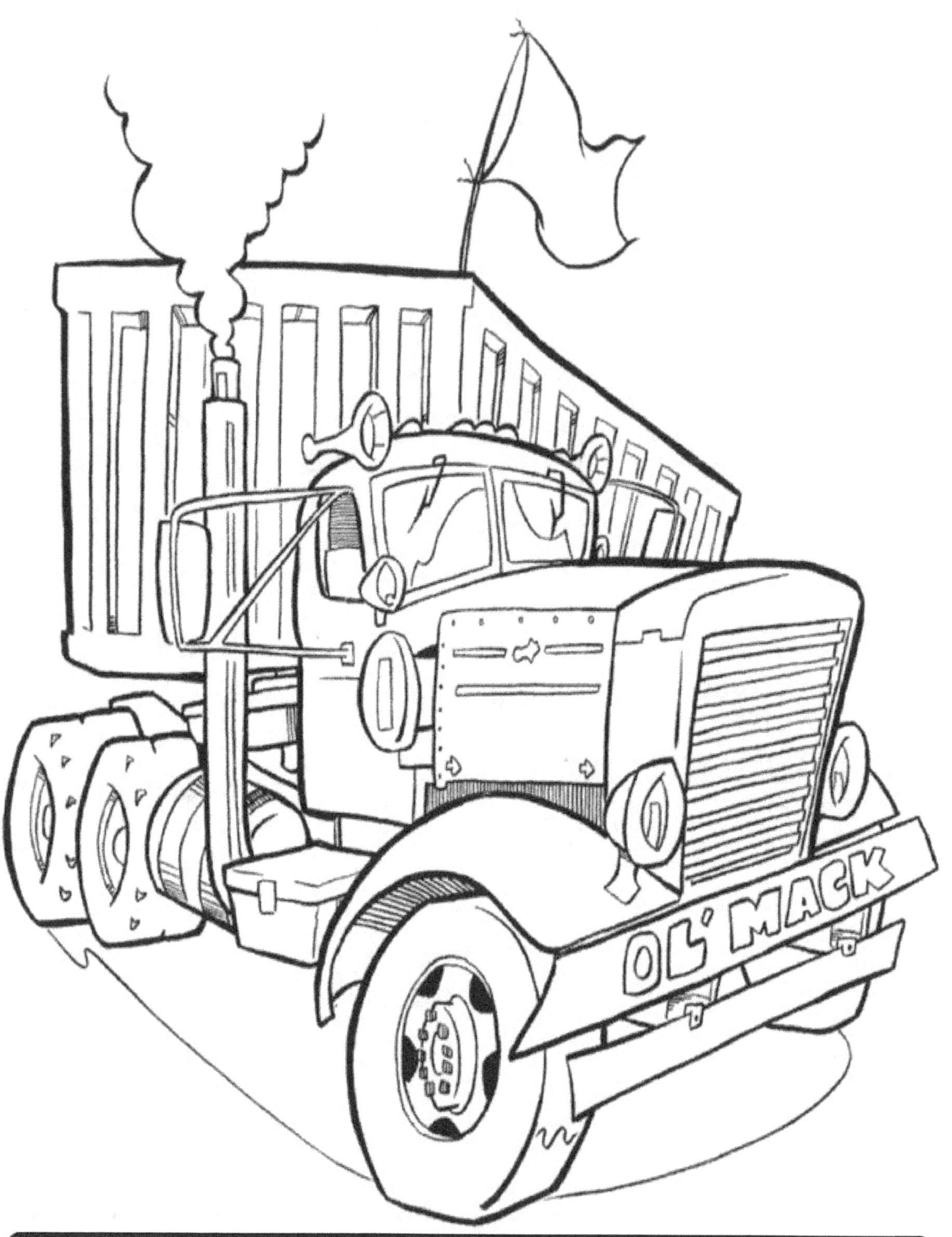

- The Average Semi-Truck is Driven
  45 Thousand Miles per Year

- That's Enough to Drive Across the U.S.
  15 Times! Road Trip!

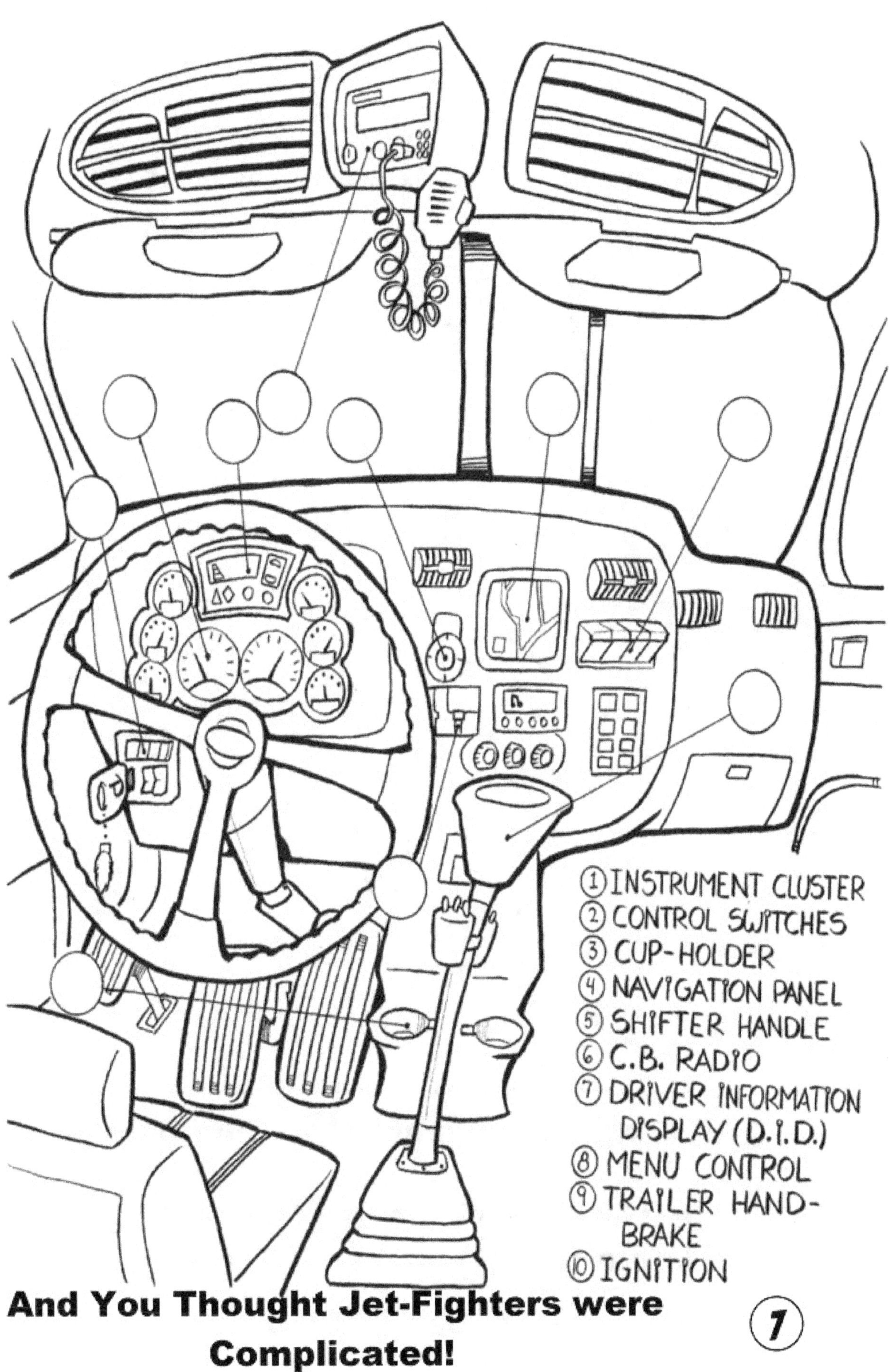

And You Thought Jet-Fighters were Complicated!

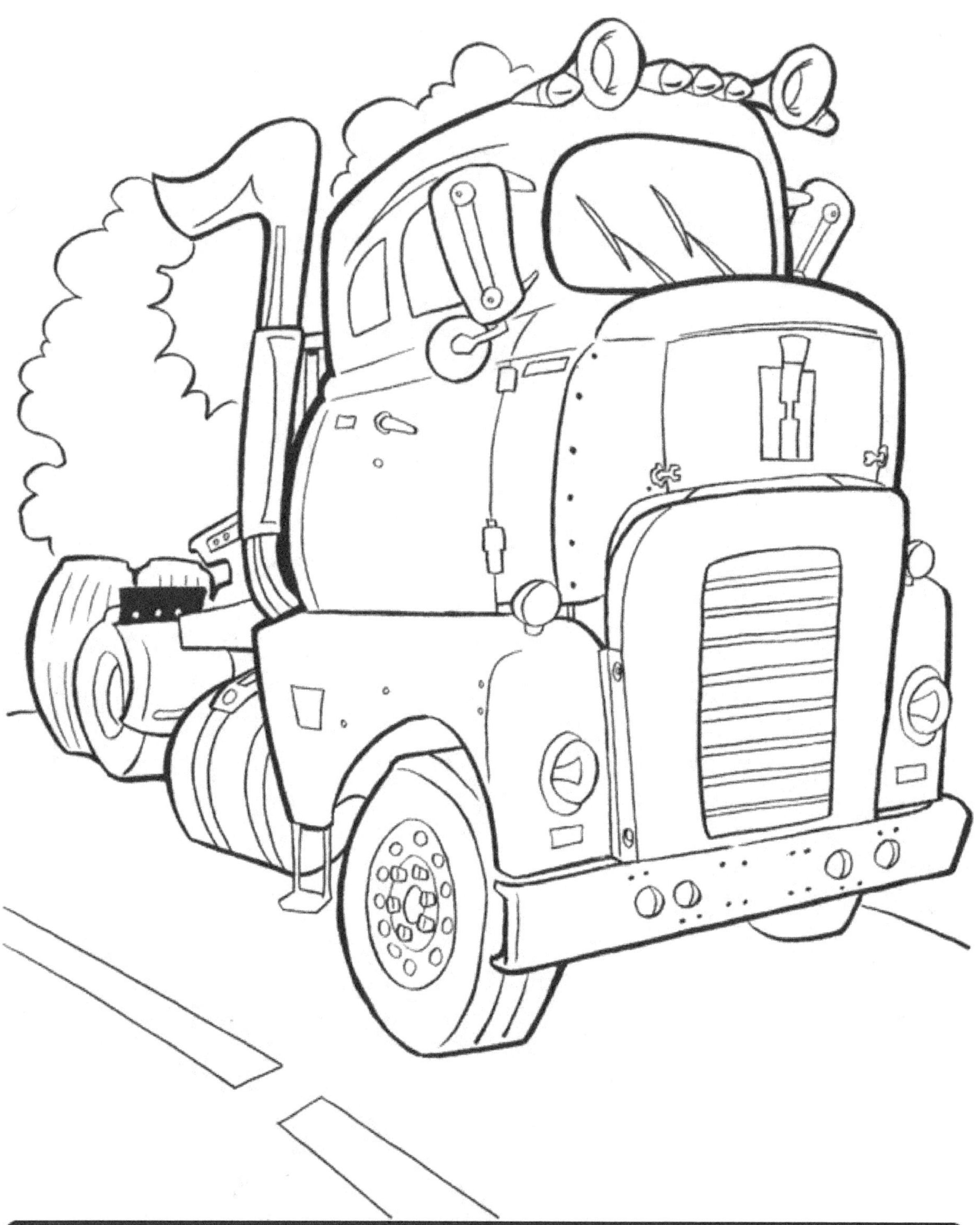

- **All Semi - Trucks are Manually Shifted**
- **It Takes 7 Weeks of Training to Learn to Drive a Tractor-Trailer! (Legally Anyway!)**

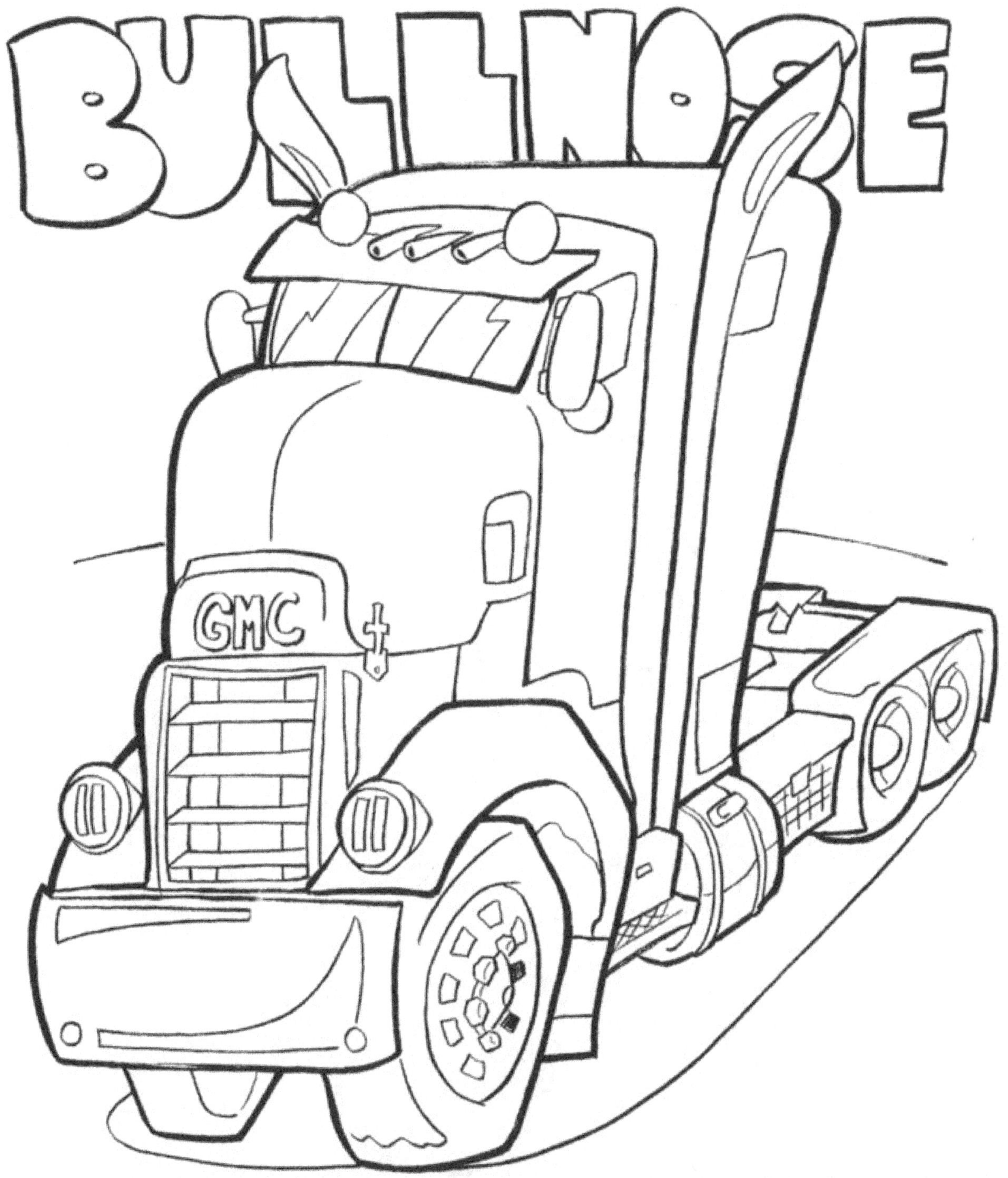

• It Takes Tractor-Trailers 2 Football Fields to Stop

• One Semi - Truck Equals the Weight of 13 of the Heaviest SUV's! "I'm Just Big Boned"

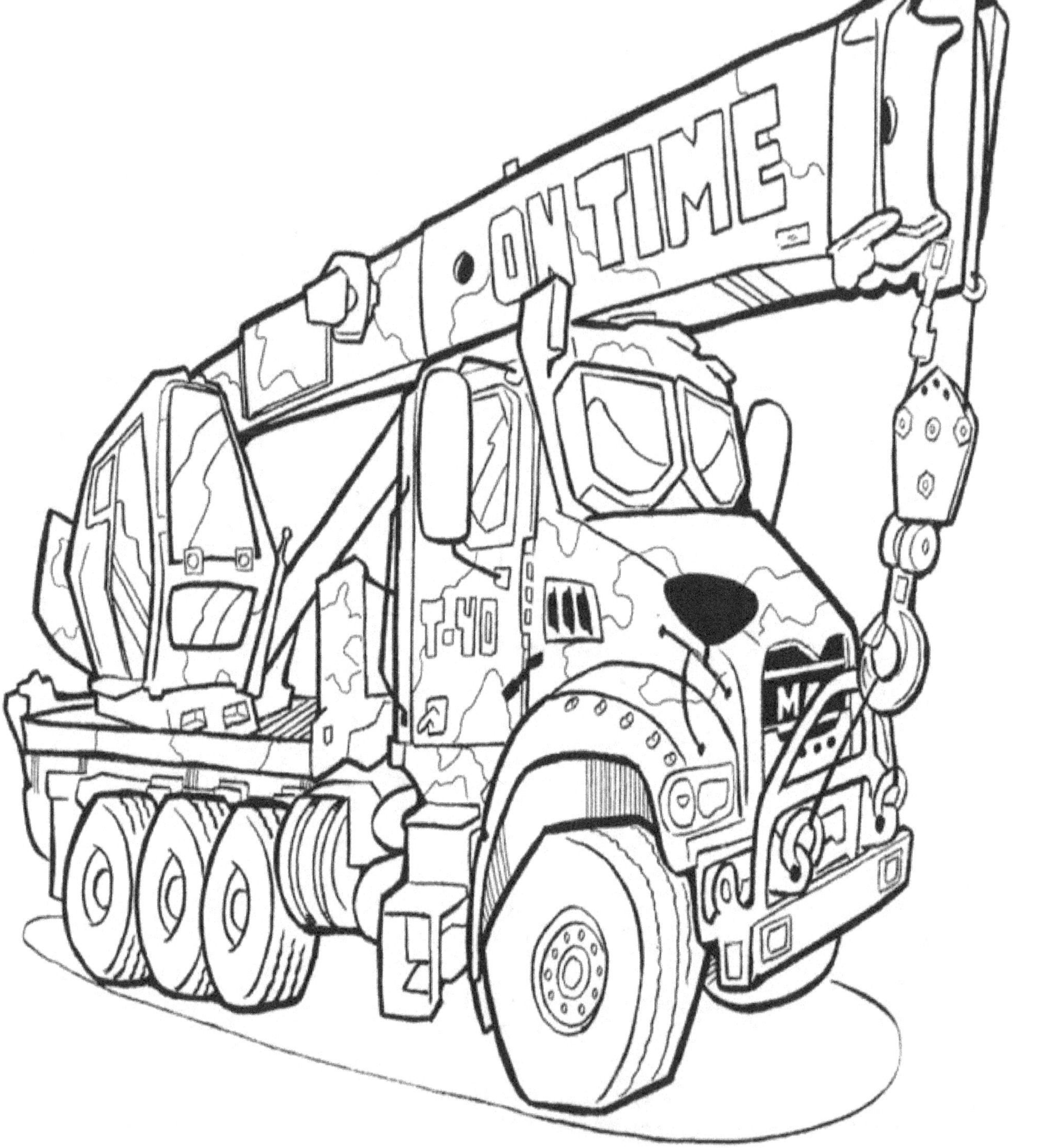

- The US Armys' "Tank Mover" Can Haul Tanks at 50 MPH! Show Off!

- "Mack Trucks" Have Been Making Military Vehicles Since 1911

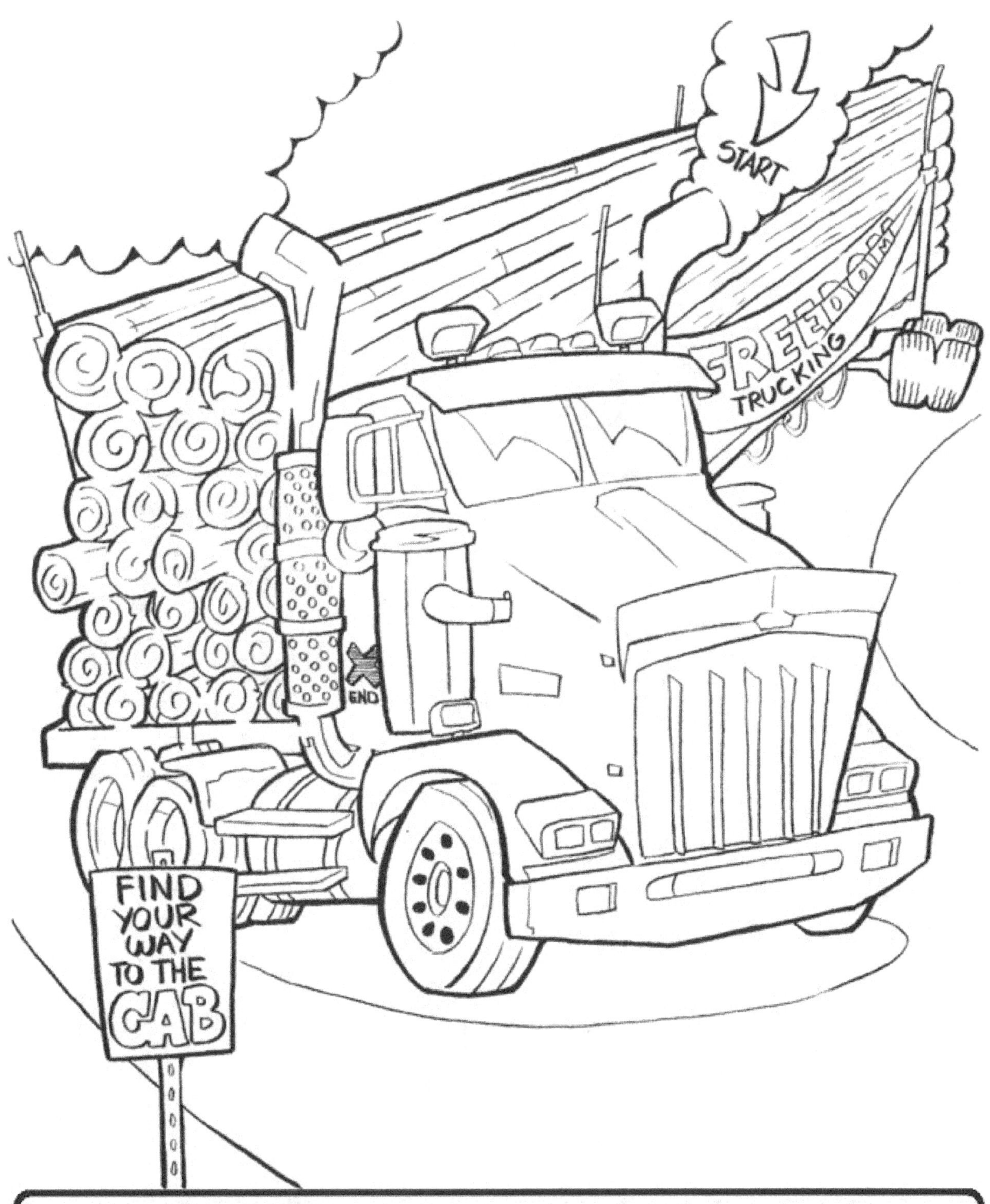

- **Peterbilt Makes the 2nd Most Popular Rig**
  We're Number 2, ♫ We're Number 2 ♫
- **An "18 Wheeler" actually Has 19 "Wheels" Counting The "5th Wheel" Trailer Hitch!**

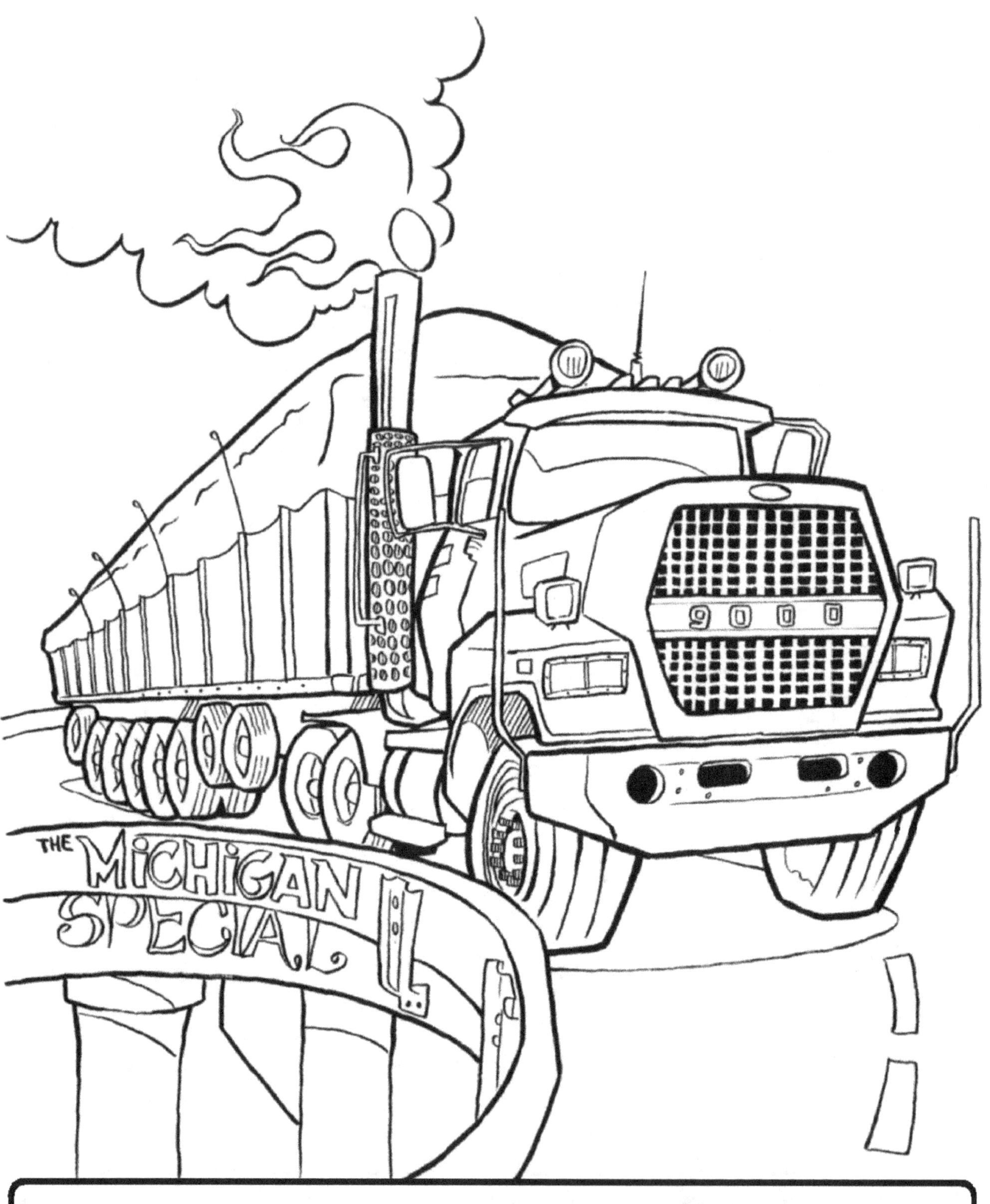

- **As of 2015 Commercial Trucks Had Traveled 280 Billion Miles!**
- **That's Like Driving to PLUTO 87 Times!! Hope There's a Rest Stop**

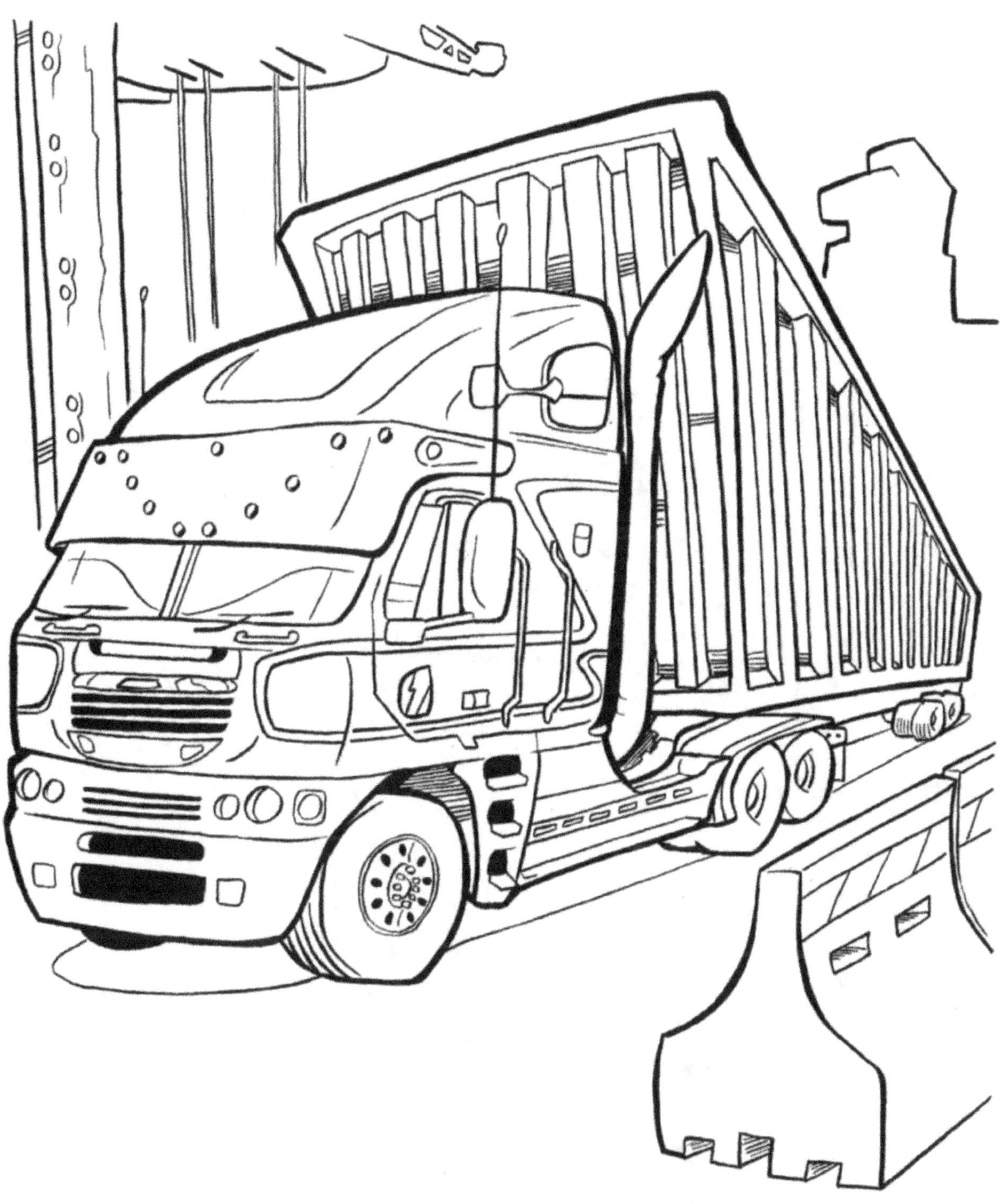

- 70% of American Goods are Transported by Big Rigs

- Container Trailers Use a "Skeleton" Frame

BOO!

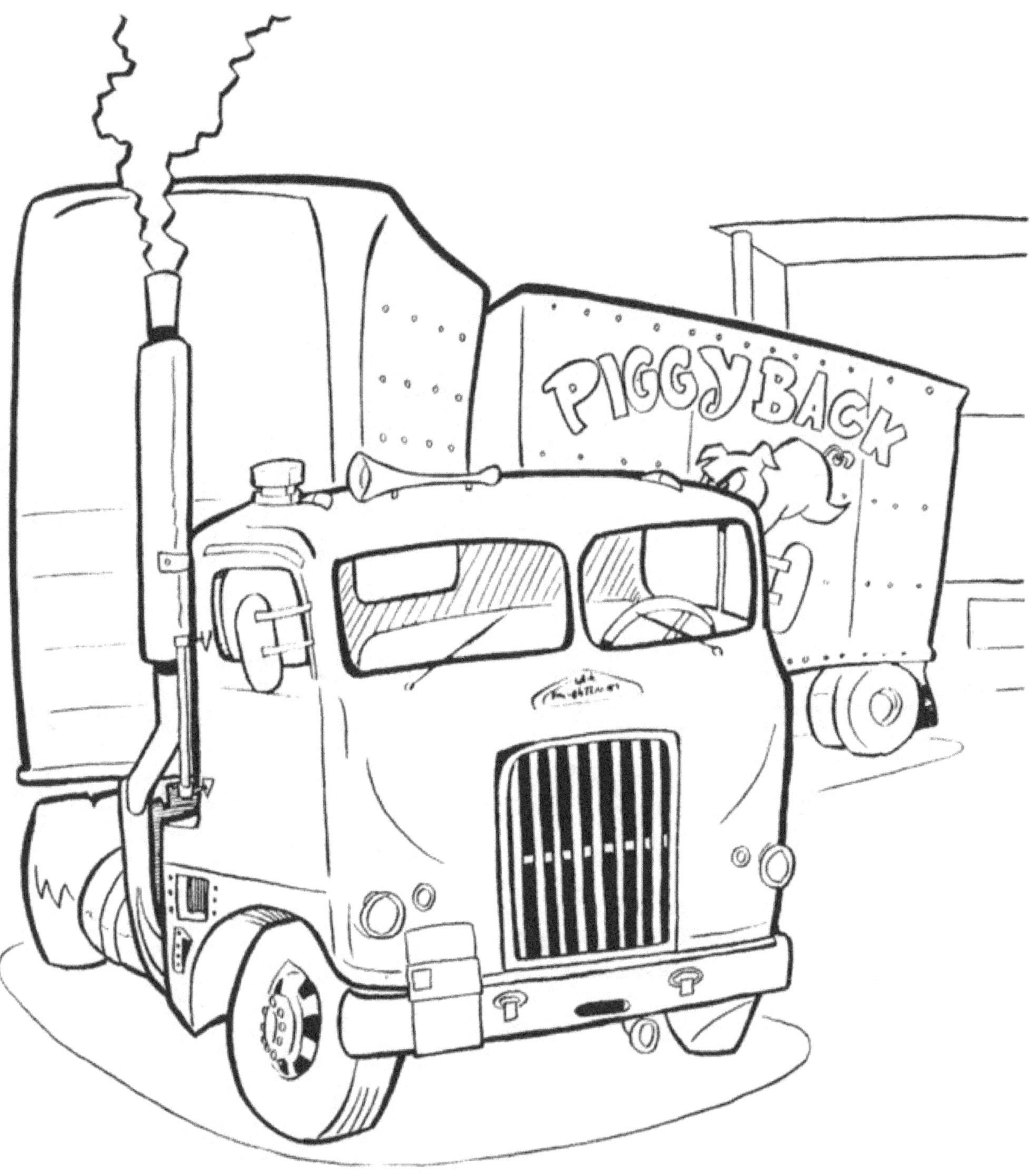

• "South Dakota Mega Trucks" Can Weigh up to 170,000 Pounds! That's 13 BIG T-Rex's!!

• Trucks Give "Piggy-Backs" One Trailer Towed Behind Another

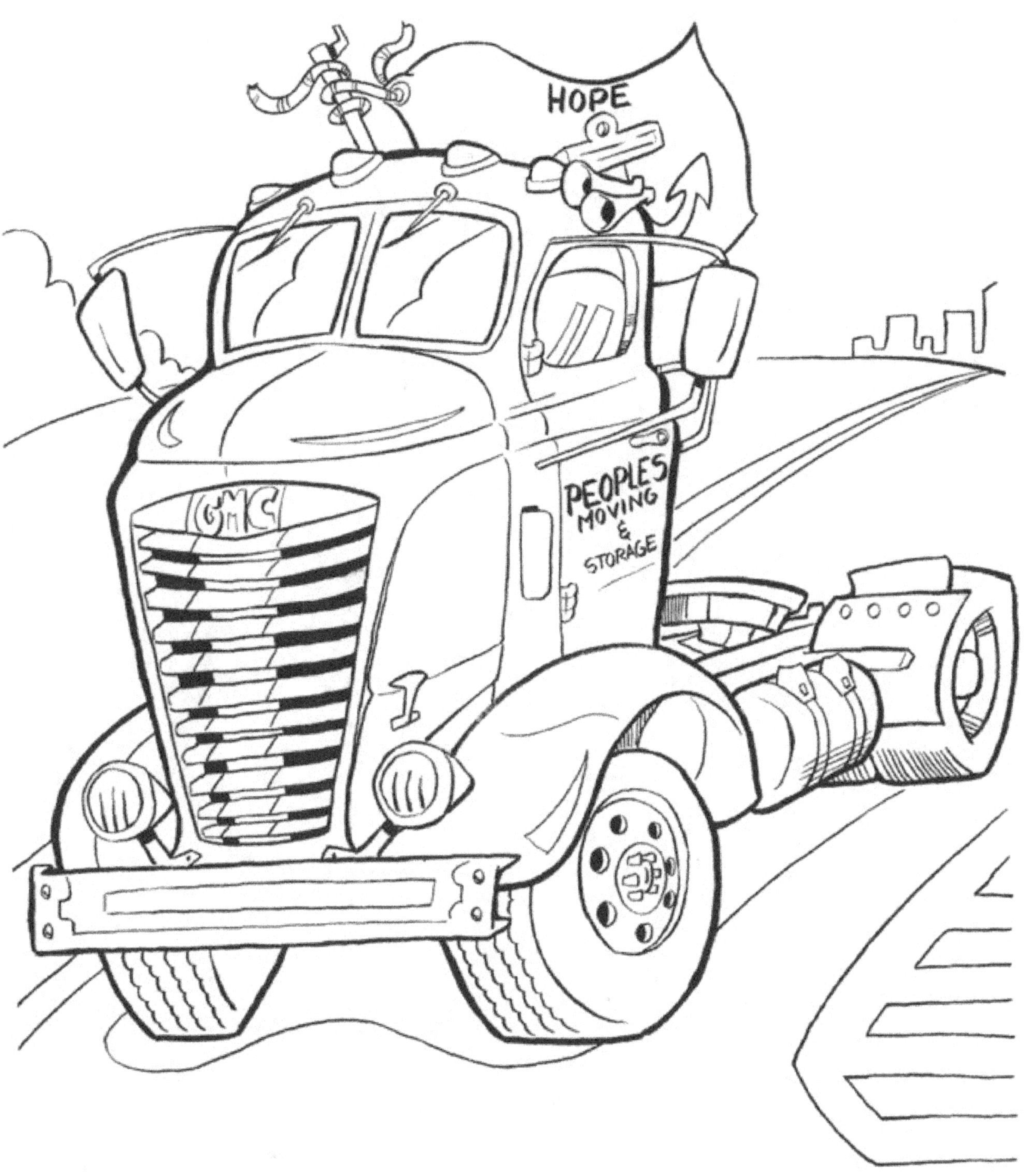

- **Commercial Trucks Transport 10 Billion Tons of Freight Per Year**
- **The "Overhead Sleeper" Was Invented in 1953 Does Sombody Need a Nap?**

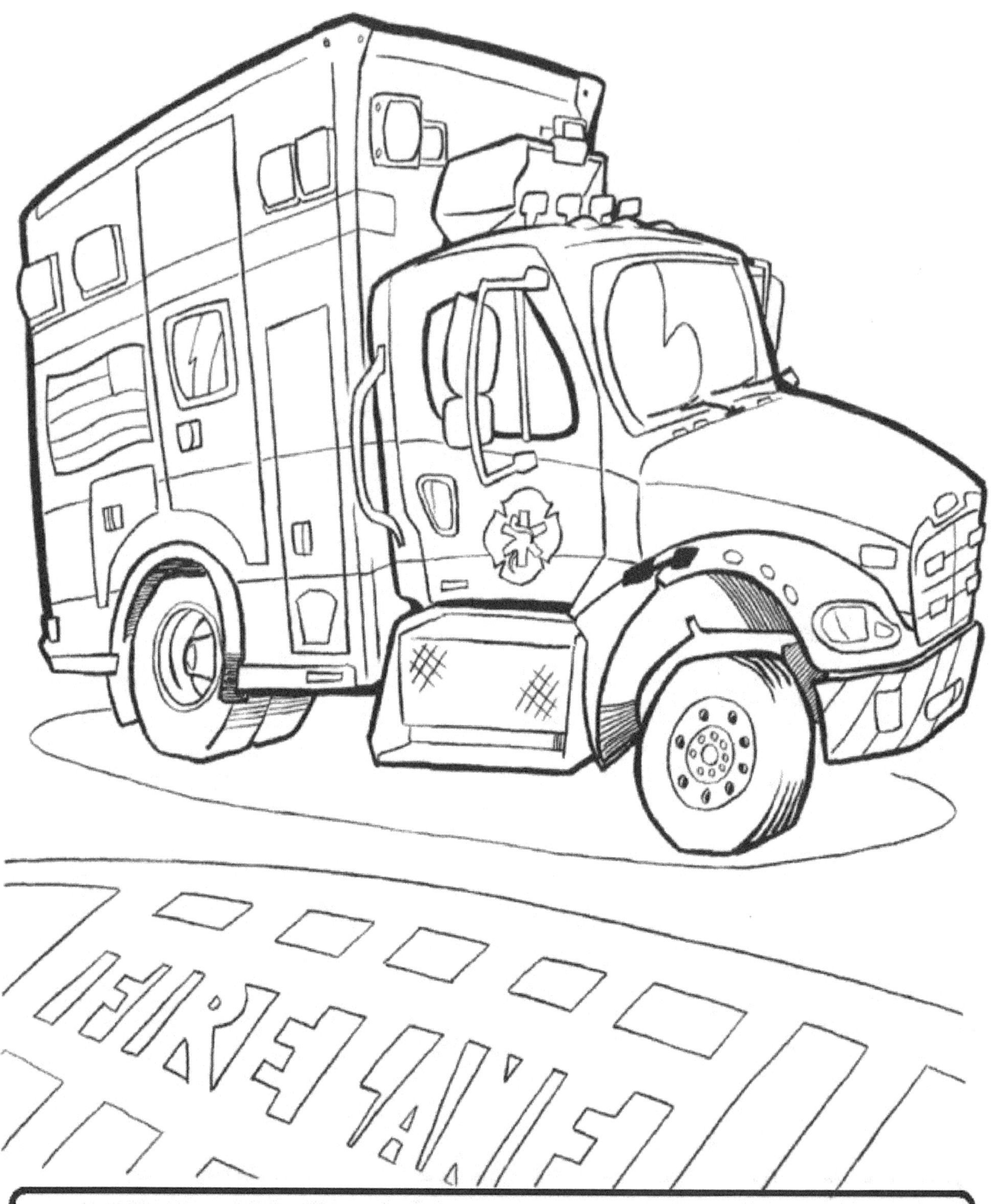

- **Of the 30 Most Dangerous Jobs, Truck Driving is 7th! CLEAR!**

- **Semi-Trucks Use Many Safety Features - Like A Collision Avoidance System!**

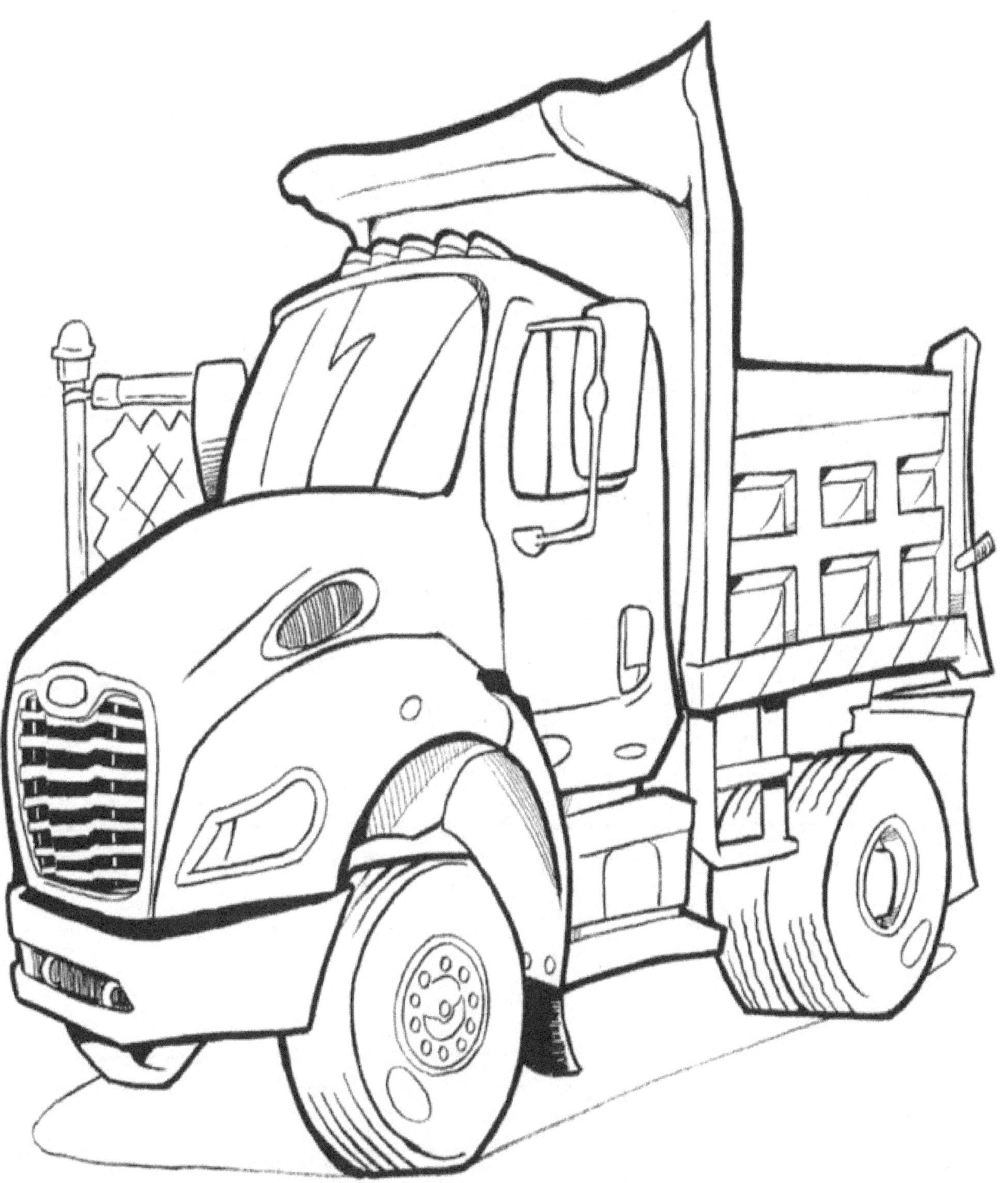

- It Takes 2 Semi-Trucks to Transport the Tires of The Caterpillar Model 797
- And The 797 Can Carry 397 Million M&M's! Talk About a "Sharing Size"!

SCRAMBLE

B5
C5
D5
E5
F4
B3
A4
E6
E3
F5
E1
F3
E4
D4
F6
F1
E2
A3
C3
B2
A1
F2
B1
C2
C6
A6
D1
C4
D2
D3
B6
C1
A2
A5
B4
D6

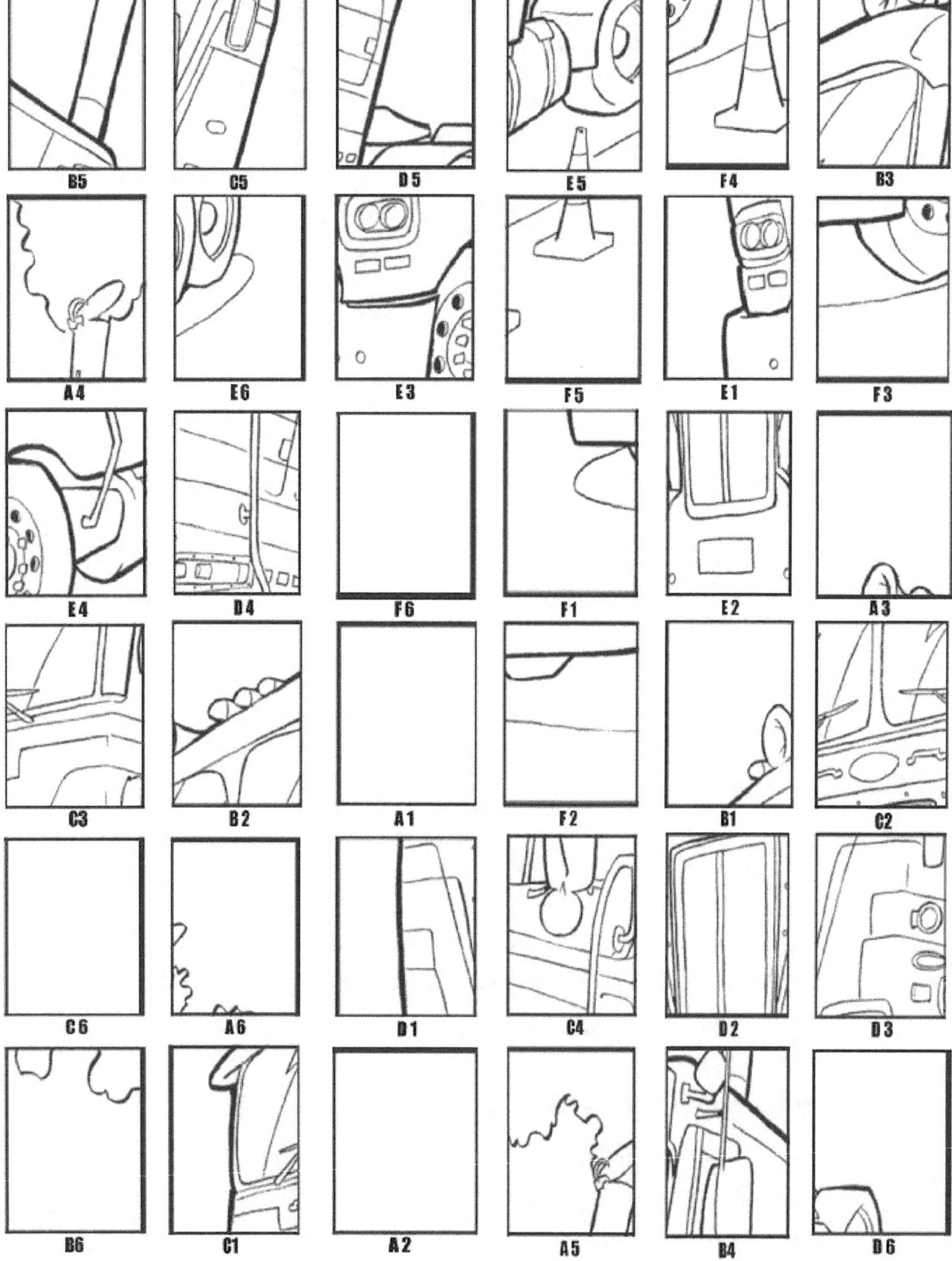

	1	2	3	4	5	6
A						
B						
C						
D						
E						
F						

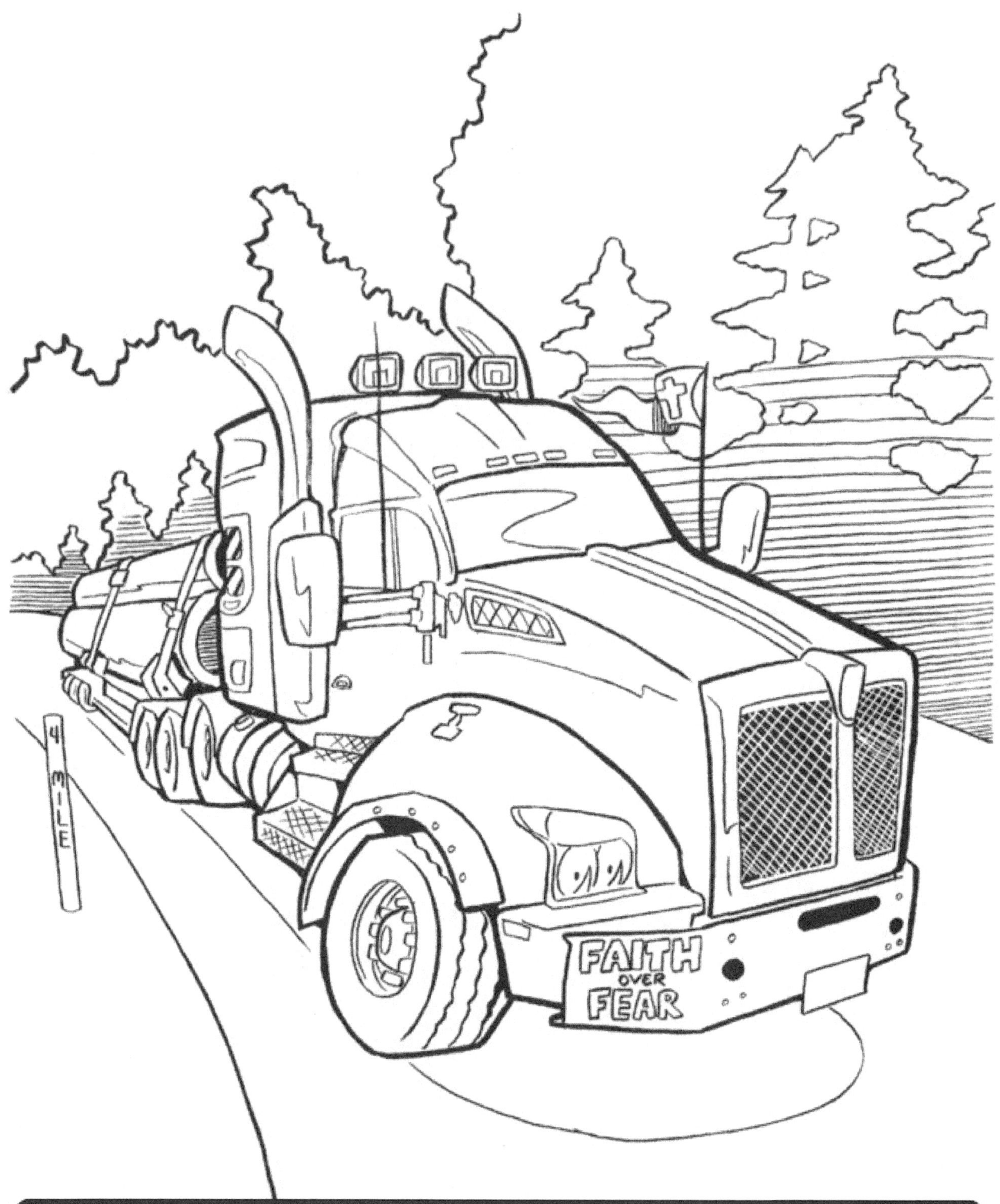

- **Specialized "Low Bed" Trailers are Used to Haul Really Tall & Really Heavy Loads**
- **Drivers Tell Weird Stories Of Things They've seen on the Road - Like the "Flaming Comet" Truck!**

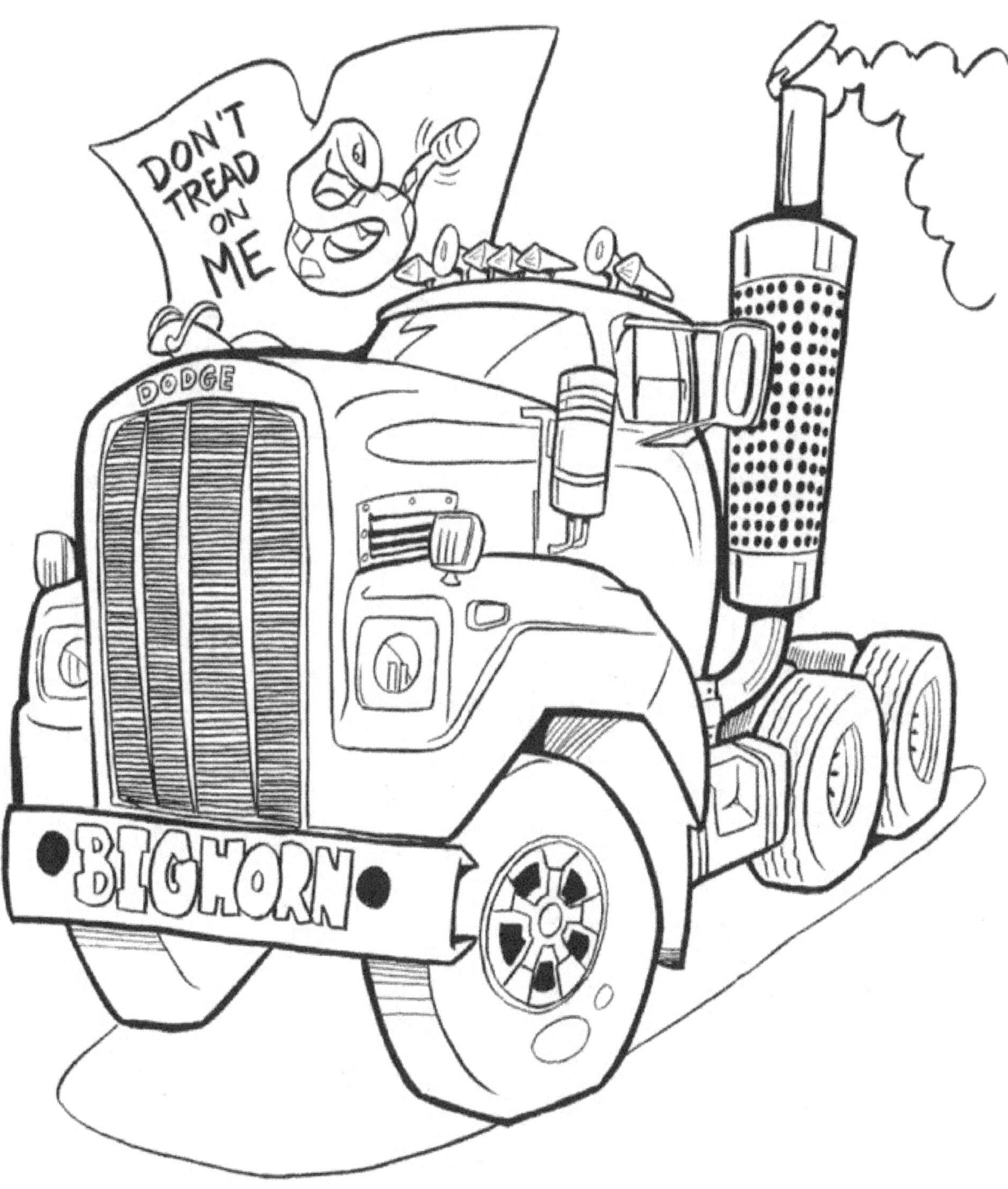

- "Big Rigs" Engines Were Designed to Run Non-Stop **- Race You!**
- The World's Longest Truck, The Hand Built "Red Giant" is 93 Feet Long!

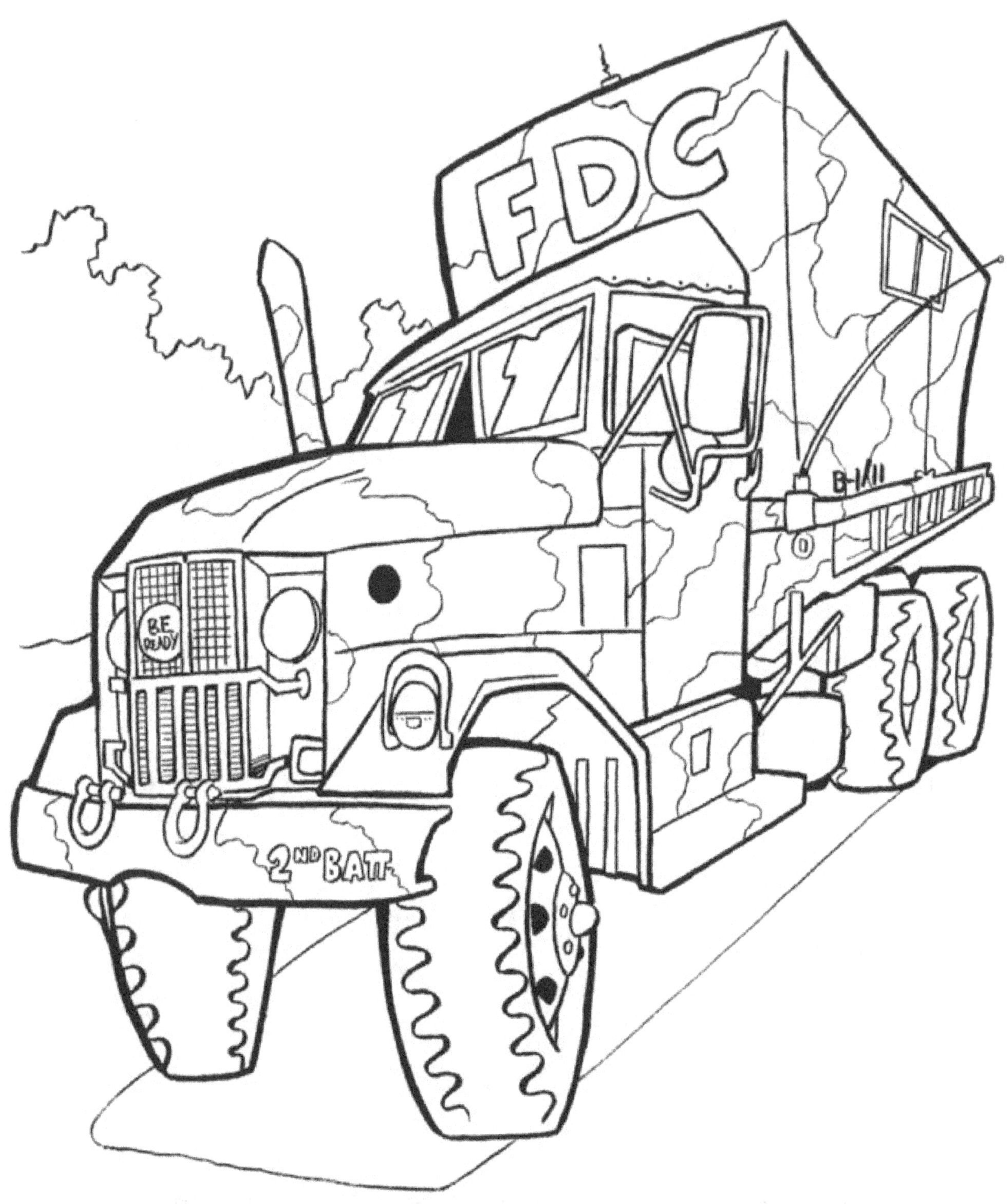

- "AMC" Who Used to Make Military Vehicles Was also a Leading Maker of Refrigerators!

- And a Man Who was One of Their Head Designers Played a 9 Year Old Girl on TV!

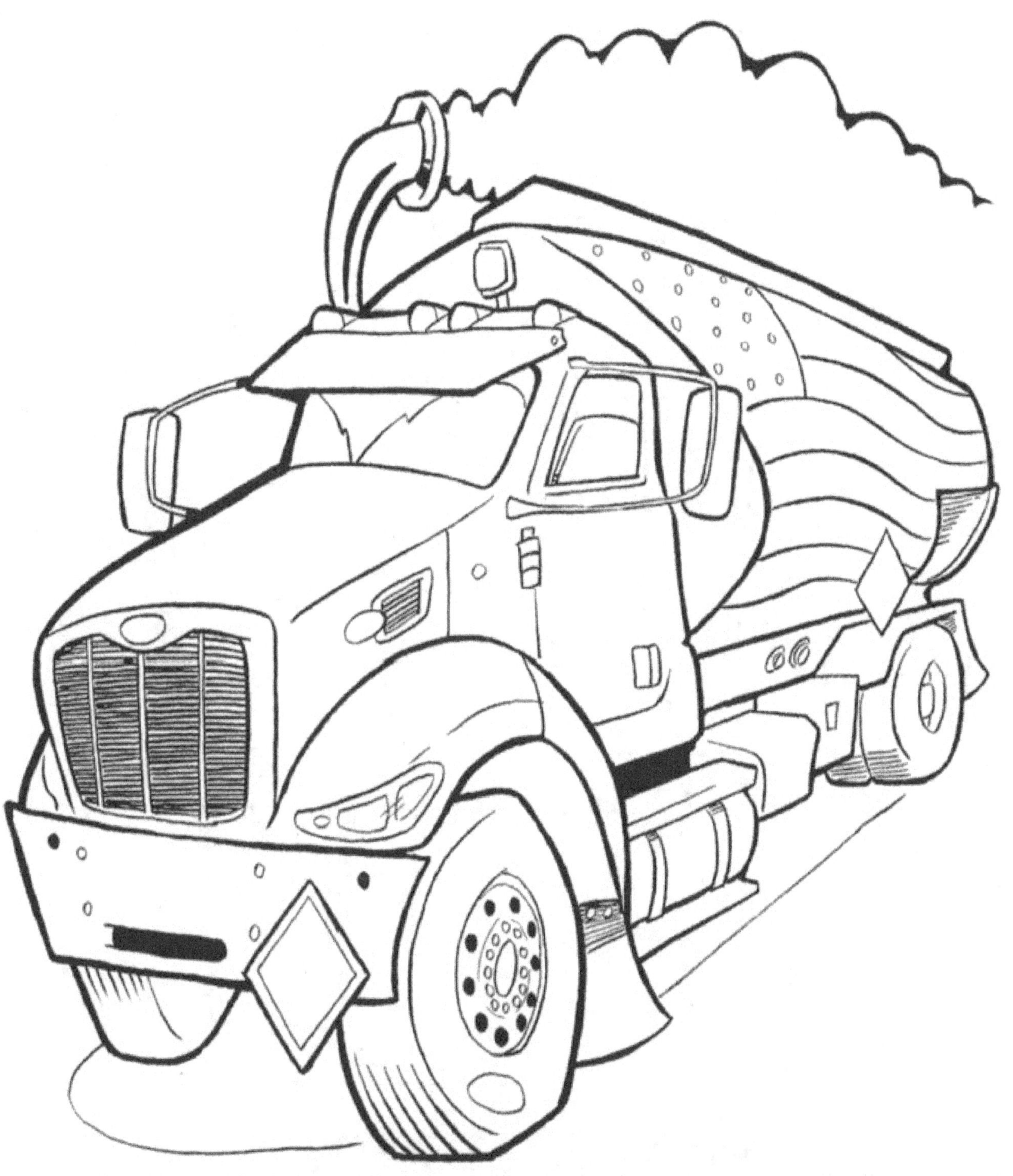

- As of 2006, Diesel Fuel is 333 Times Cleaner Than the Original Mix.
- A "Sewage" Vacuum Truck Can Hold More than 1500 Gallons in Its' Tank. What's That Smell?

FINISH LOADING THE TRUCK

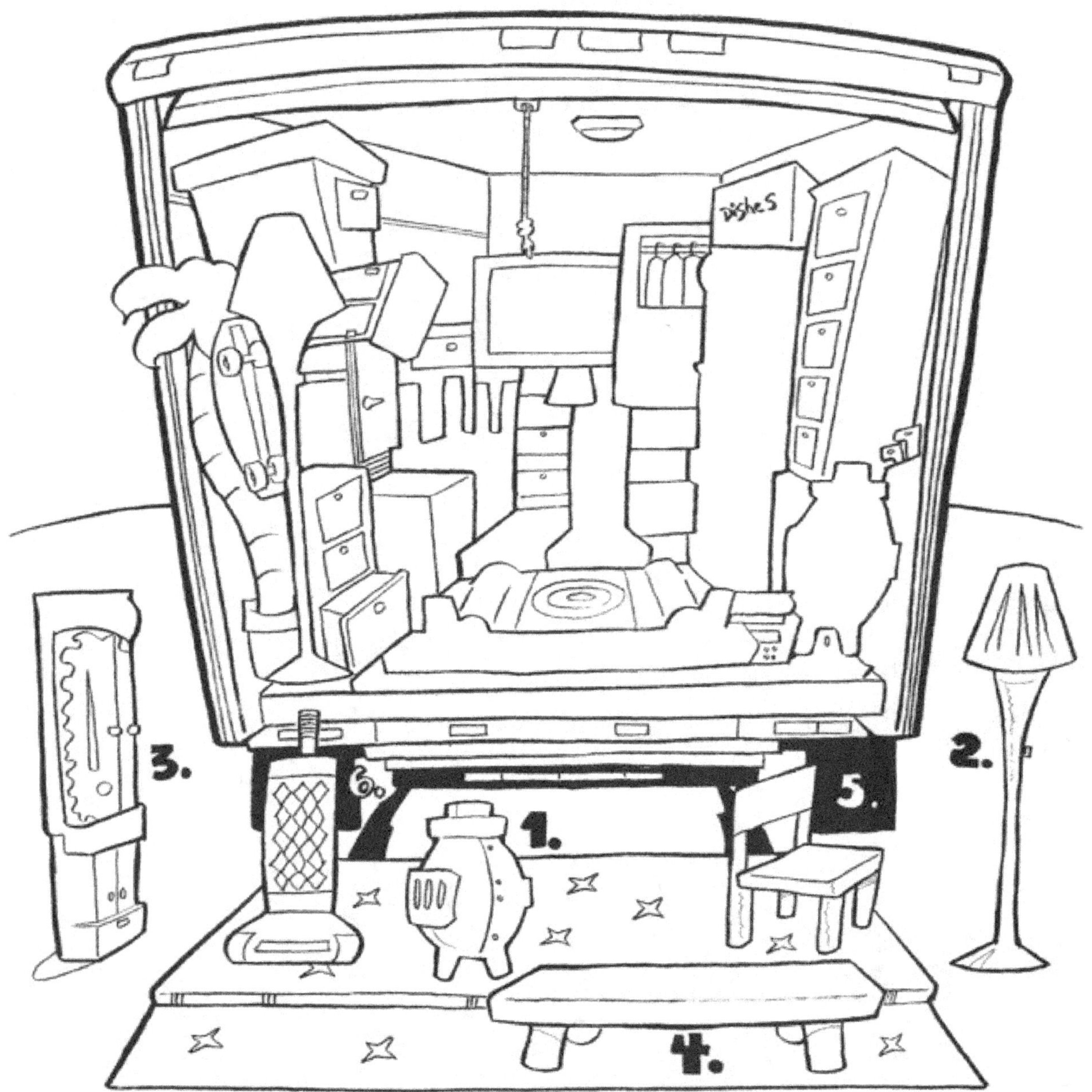

WHERE DO THEY FIT?

- **Trailers Used to Move Furniture Are Known as "Dry Van's" ('Cuz They keep Everything Cozy & Dry!)**

- **6% of Truck Drivers are Women!**

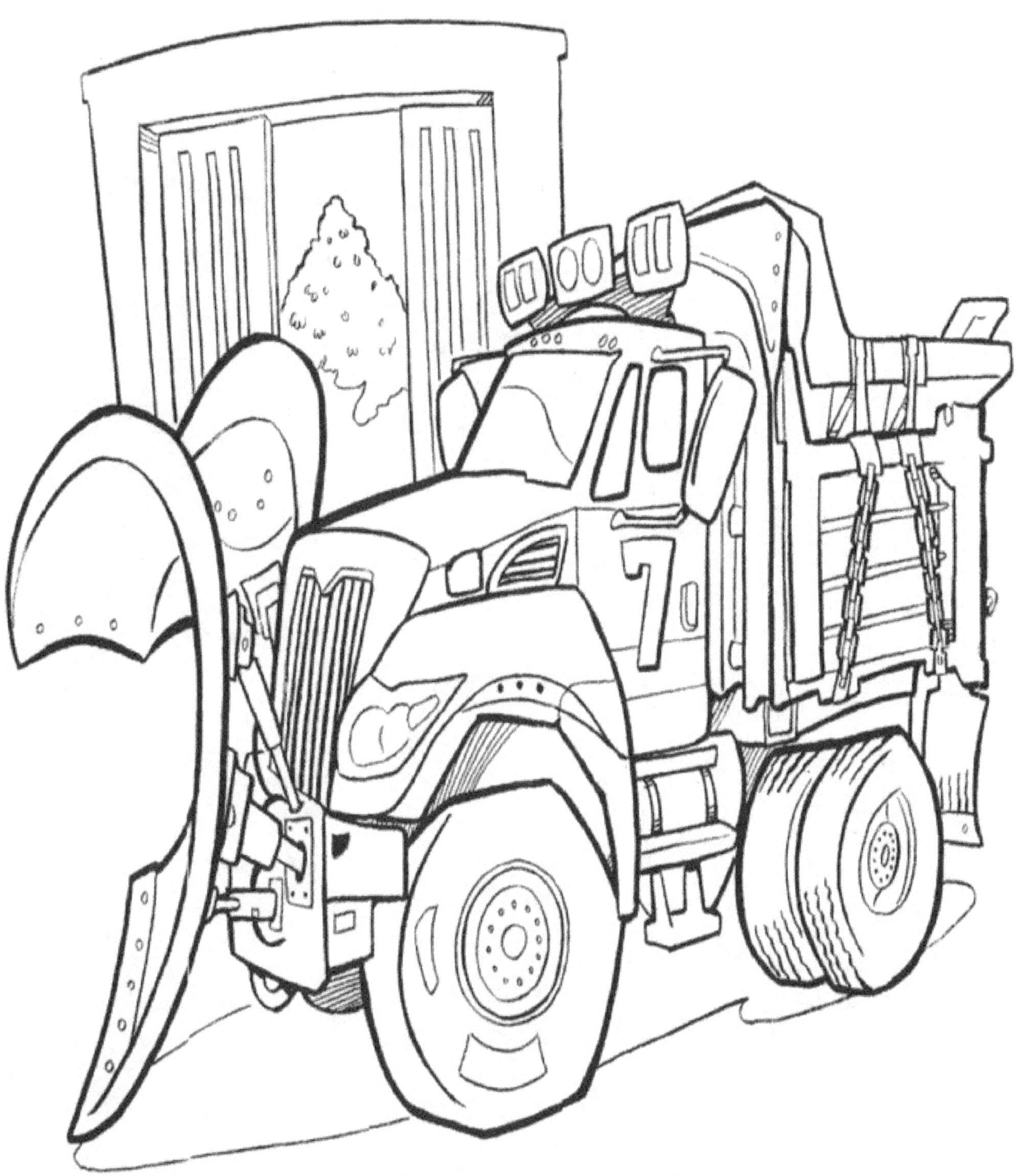

- The First Snowplow Took 31 Years to Develop!
- A Single Snow Storm can Have the Energy of 120 Atom Bombs!

Radioactive Snow Day, Anyone?

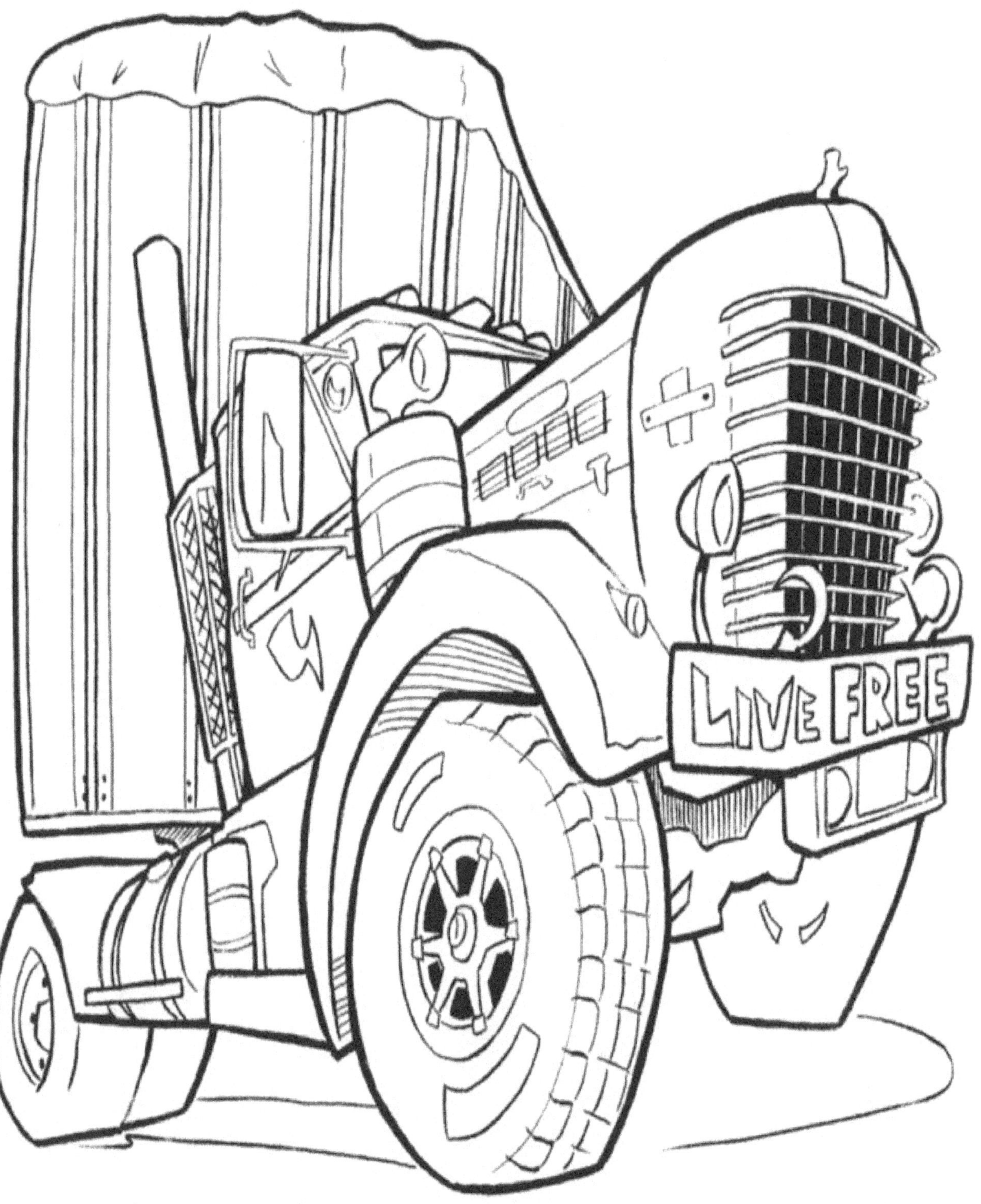

- Tractor - Trailers are Called "Rigs" in Reference to the Original Cargo Haulers - -Sailing Ships
- Early Farm Trucks Doubled as Tractors! Hope They Got Overtime

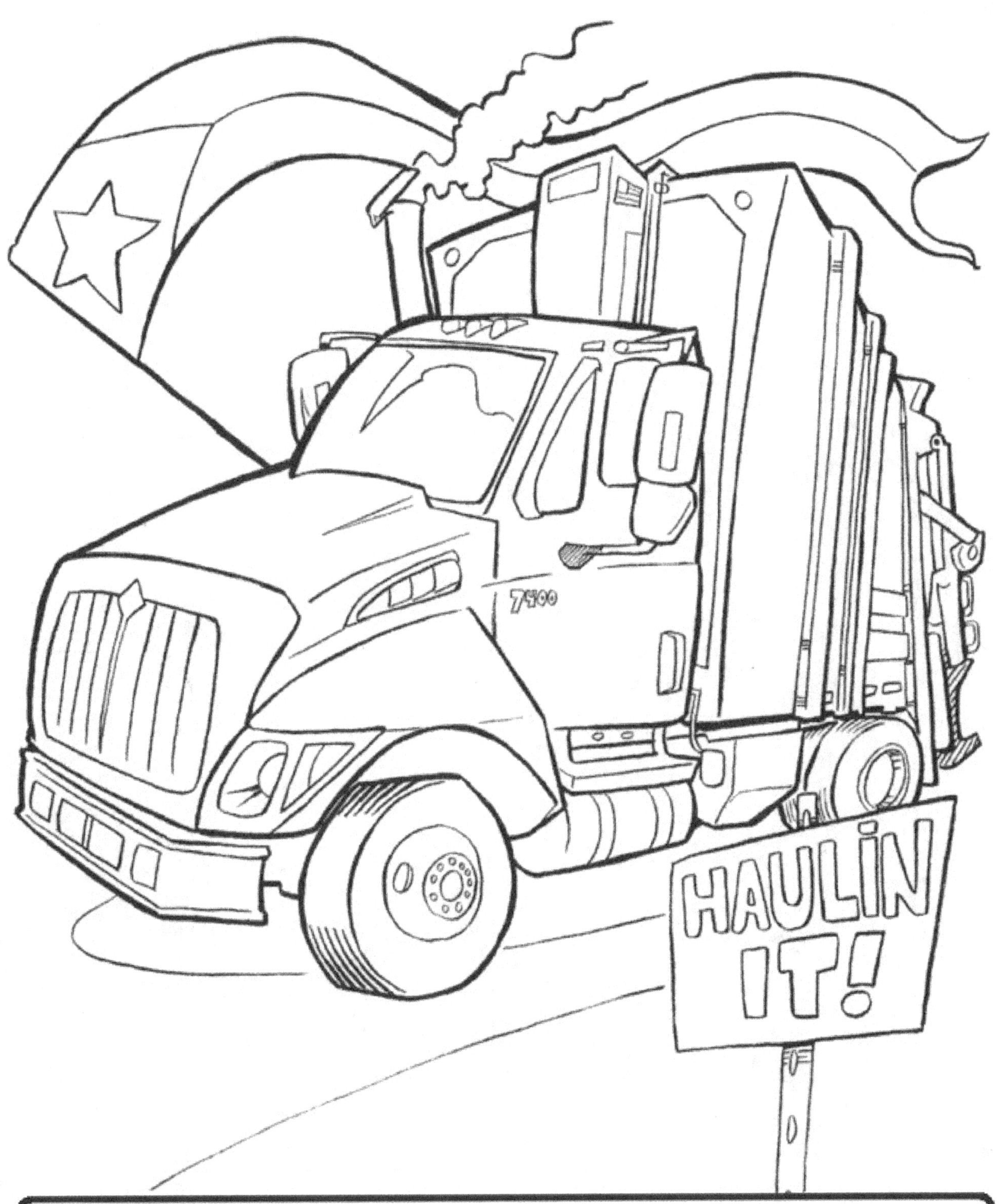

- The First "Rear-Loading" Garbage Truck was Used in 1920's New York

- The First "Dumpster" Trucks - in the 1930's (Boy are my Lifting Arms Tired)

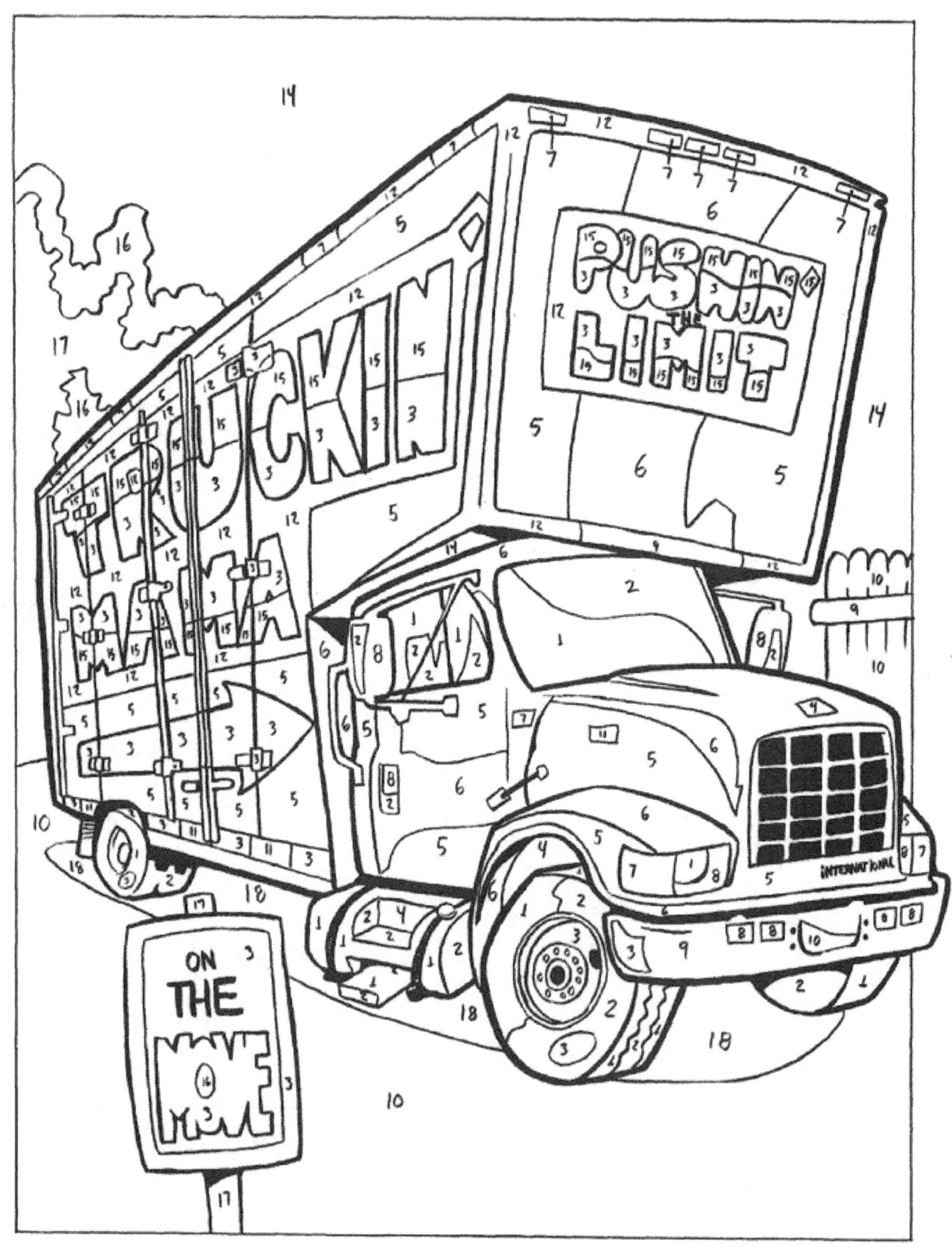

1. Light Grey 2. Dark Grey 3. White 4. Black 5. Blue
6. Dark Blue 7. Orange 8. Silver 9. Tan 10. Light Brown
11. Red 12. Yellow 13. Purple 14. Light Blue 15. Pink
16. Light Green 17. Dark Green 18. Dark Brown

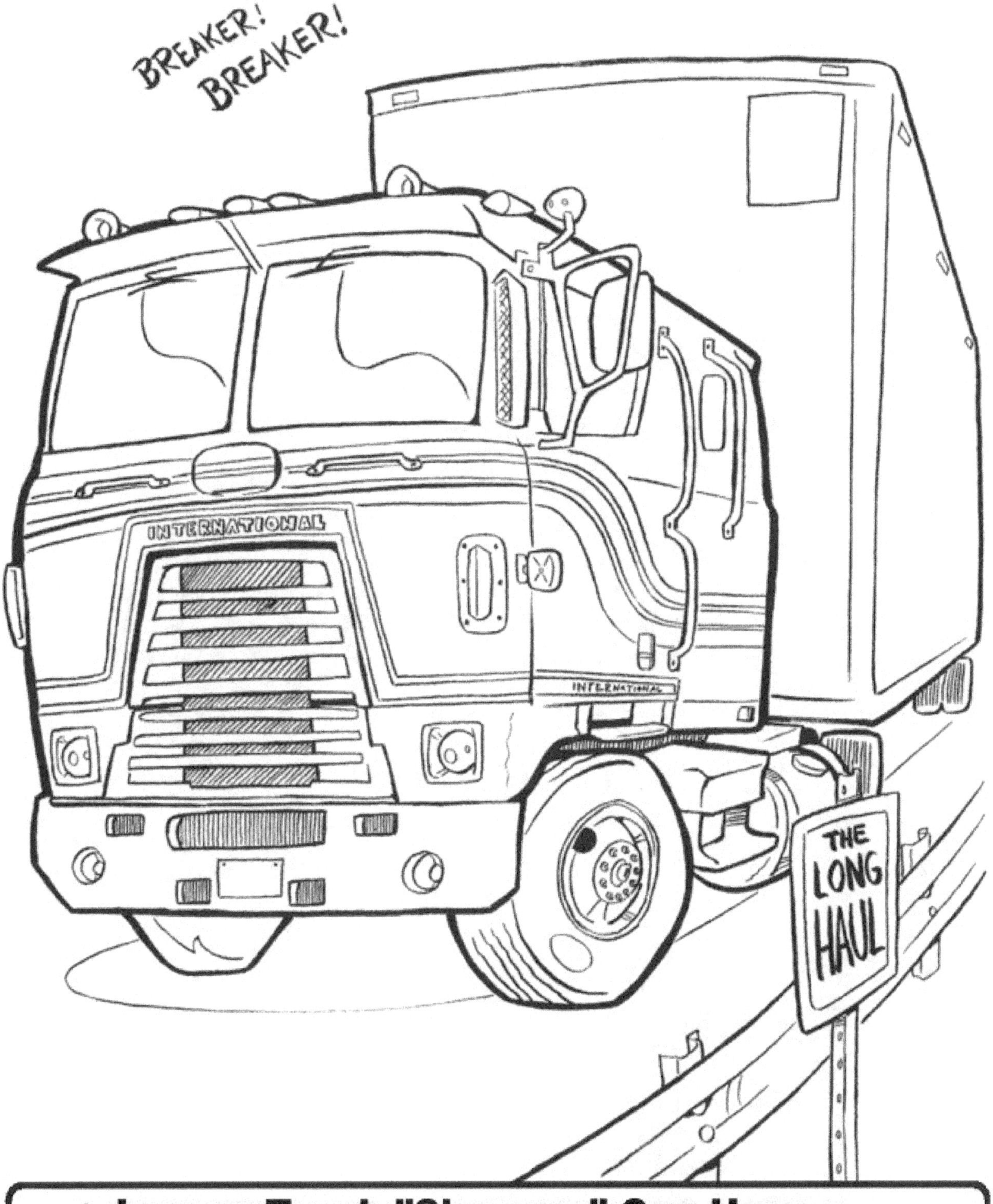

- **Luxury Truck "Sleepers" Can Have a Bathroom with Shower & a Kitchenette!**
- **Freightliner's "Aerocab" Converts into a Living Room!**

Go Ahead, Have a Few Friends Over

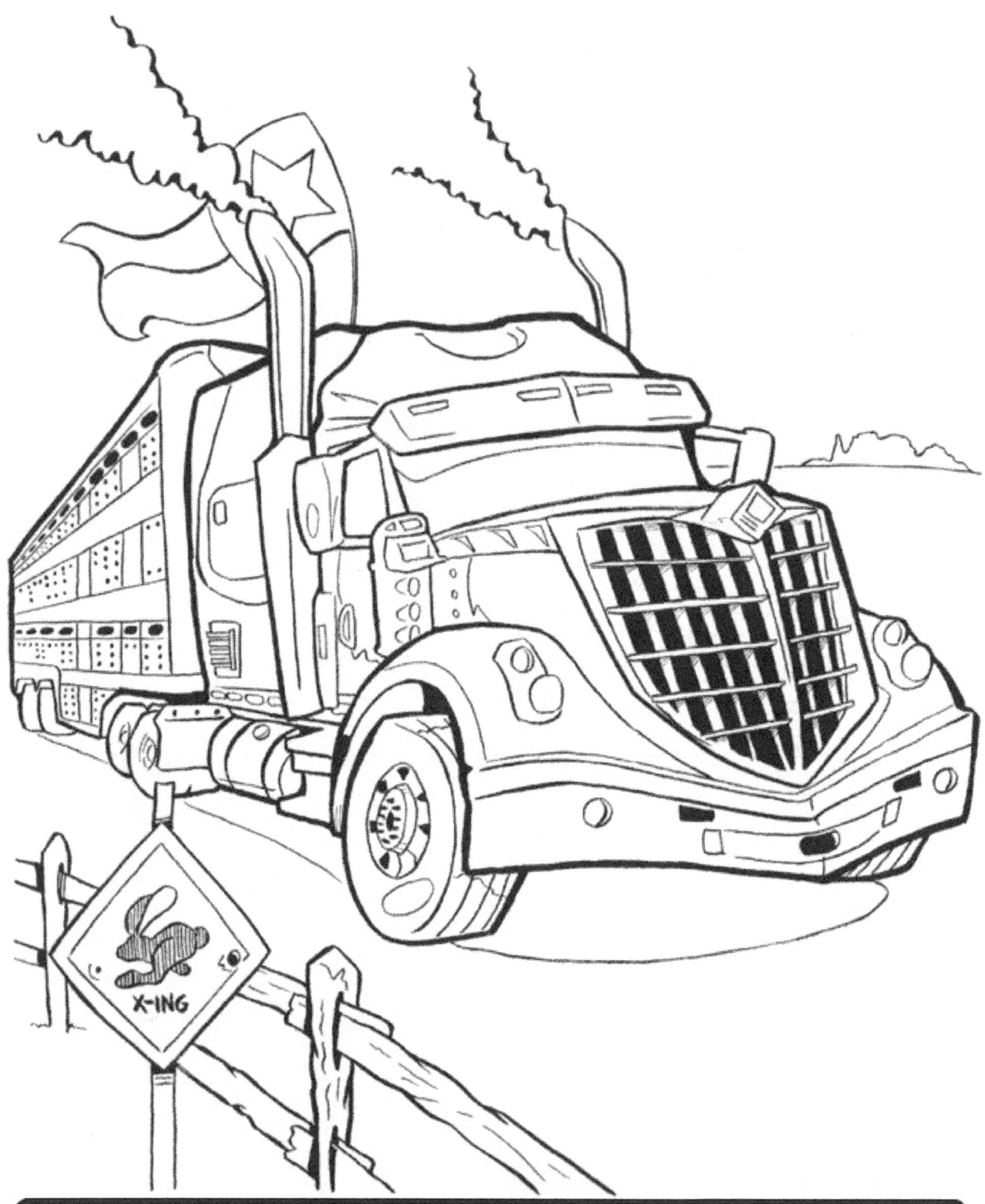

- The International "LoneStar" is the Most Powerful Commercial Truck in the US
- Semi-Trucks can have 18 Gears - One for Every Wheel! But Many Truckers Prefer 13 Gears. Must be Their Lucky Number!

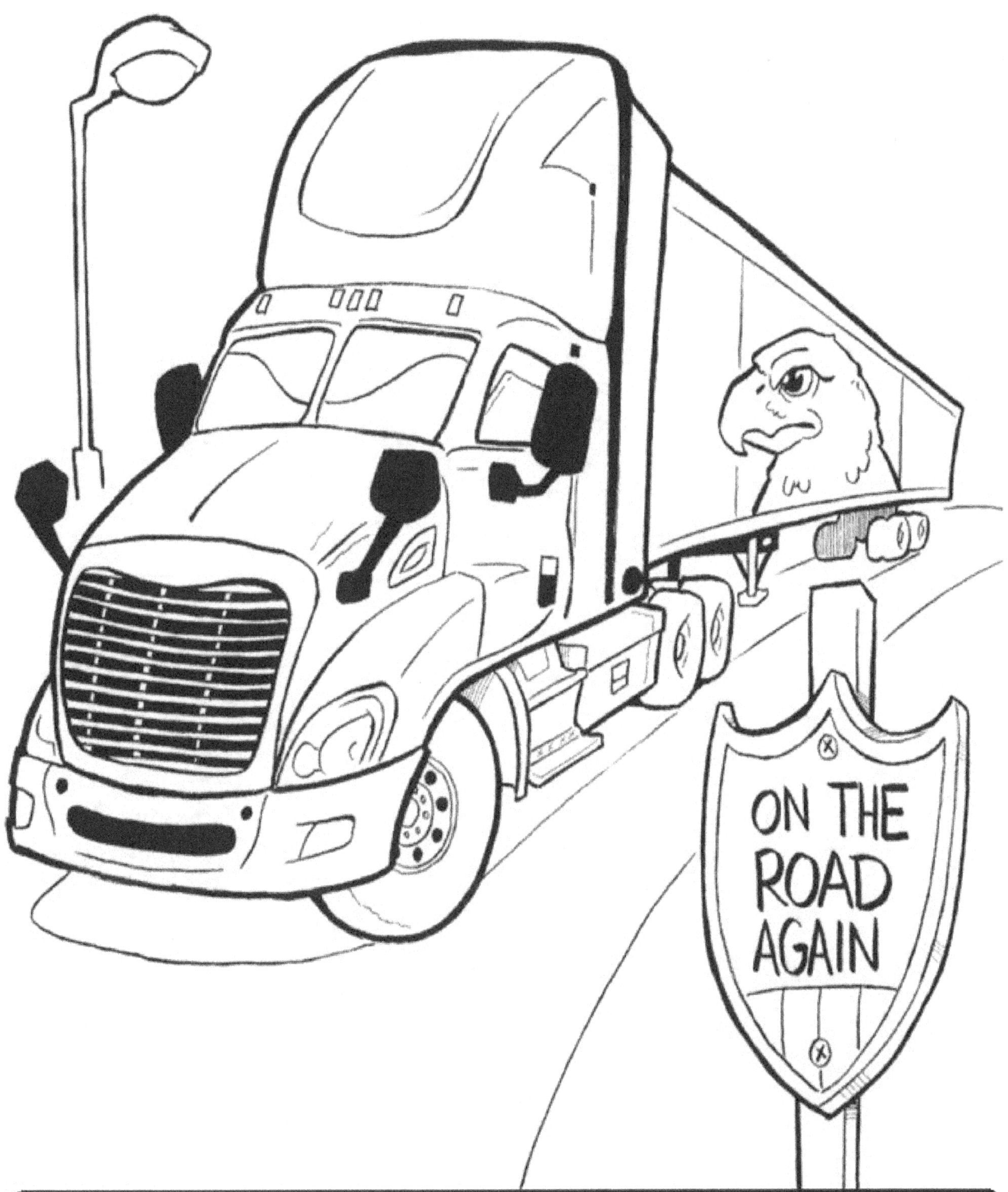

- Tractor - Trailers Can be Up to 75 Feet Long!

- The Peterbilt Model 579 Has the Most Spacious Sleeper Cabs Don't Fall Out of Bed!

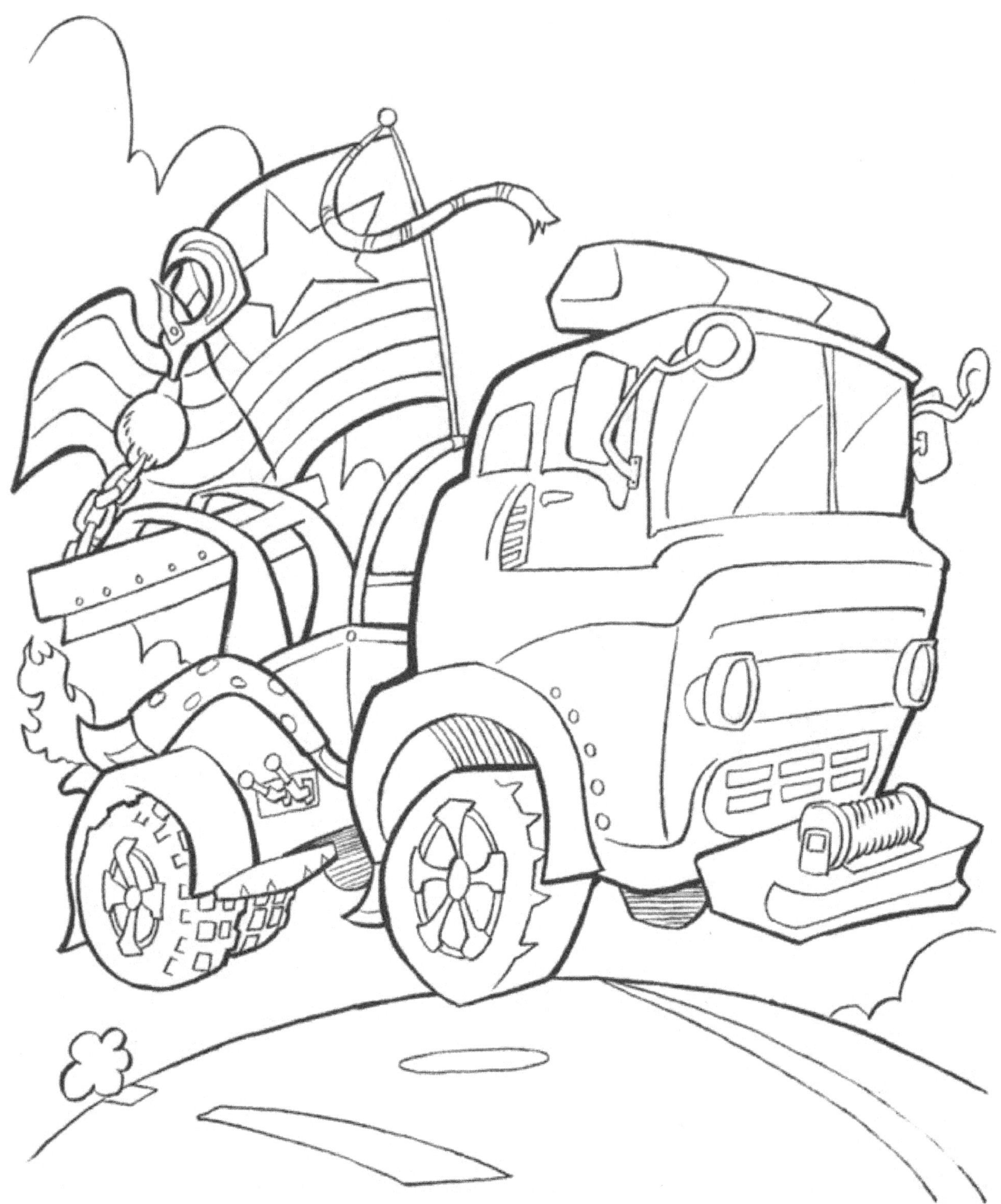

- **The Tow Truck Was Invented in Tennessee, in 1915!**
- **The Same Year AAA Started Offering Roadside Assistance**

"It's Only Flat on the Bottom!"

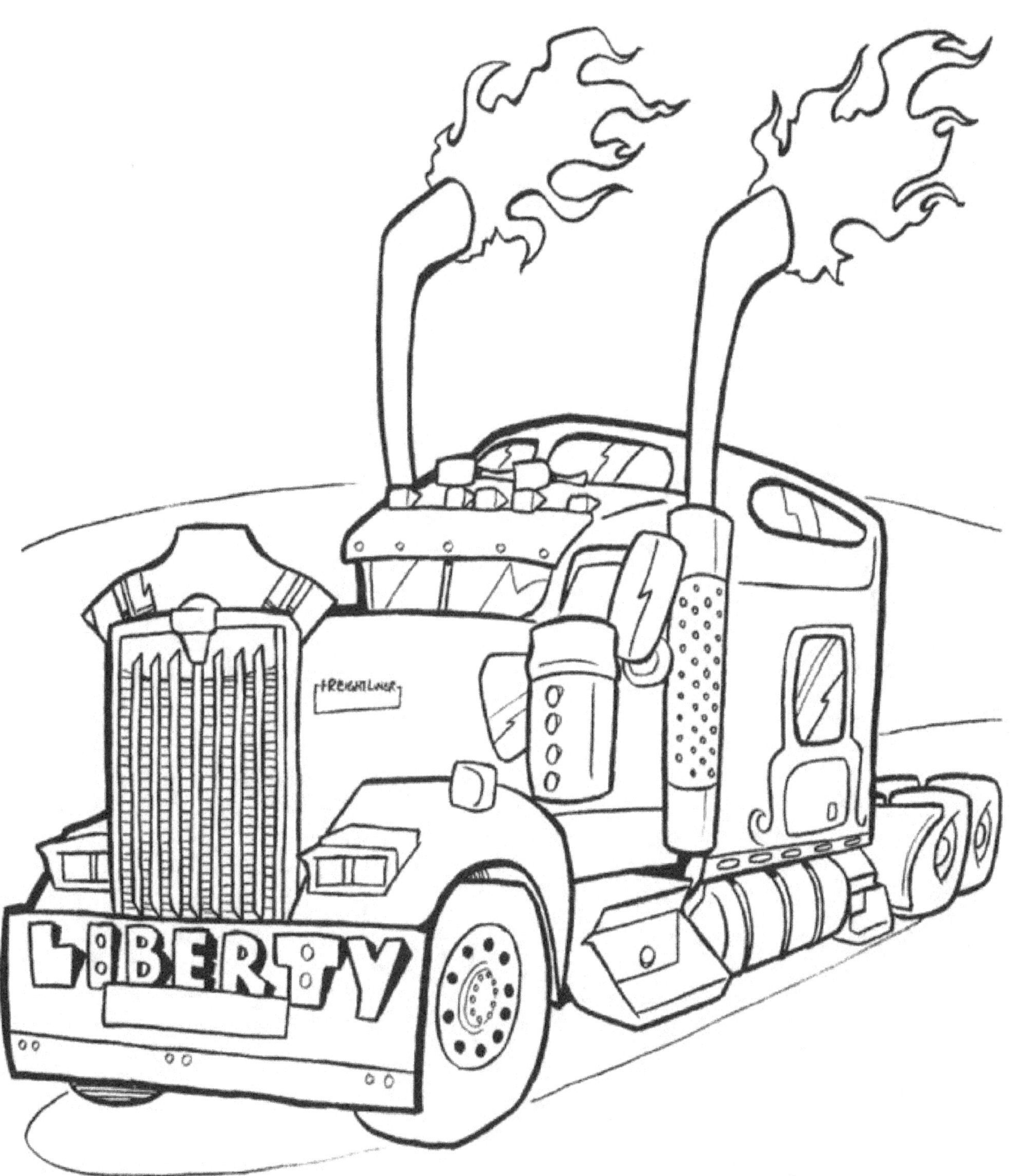

- The Fuel Tanks of a Semi Truck Hold Between 100 & 400 Gallons!
- As of 2012, Freightliner is the Most Popular Truck

And the Crown Goes to....

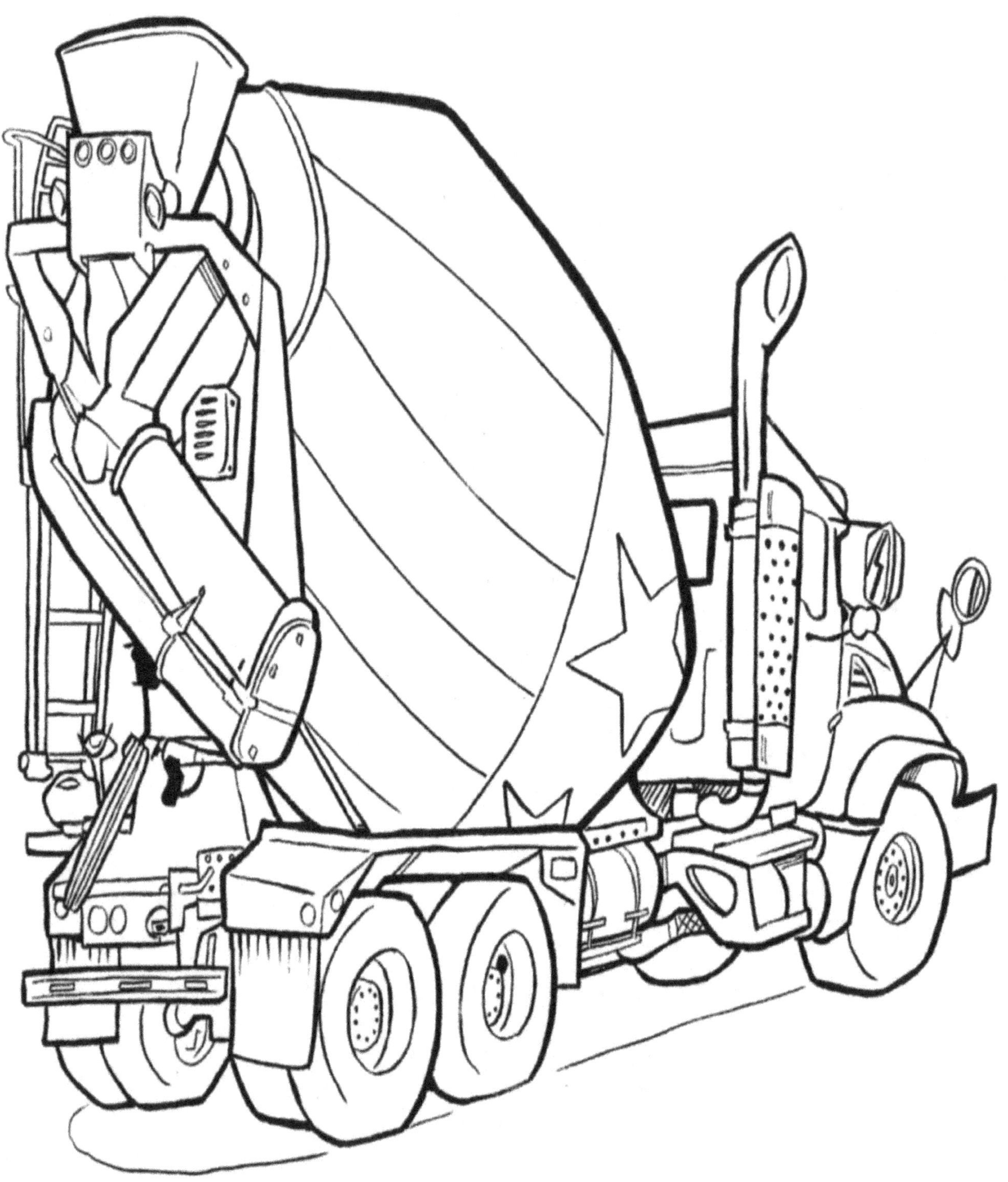

- Some "Mud Flaps" are Aerodynamically designed to Decrease Drag!
- Concrete "Ears" Designed During WW II Could Hear a Plane 27 Miles Away! Talk About "Hard" of Hearing!

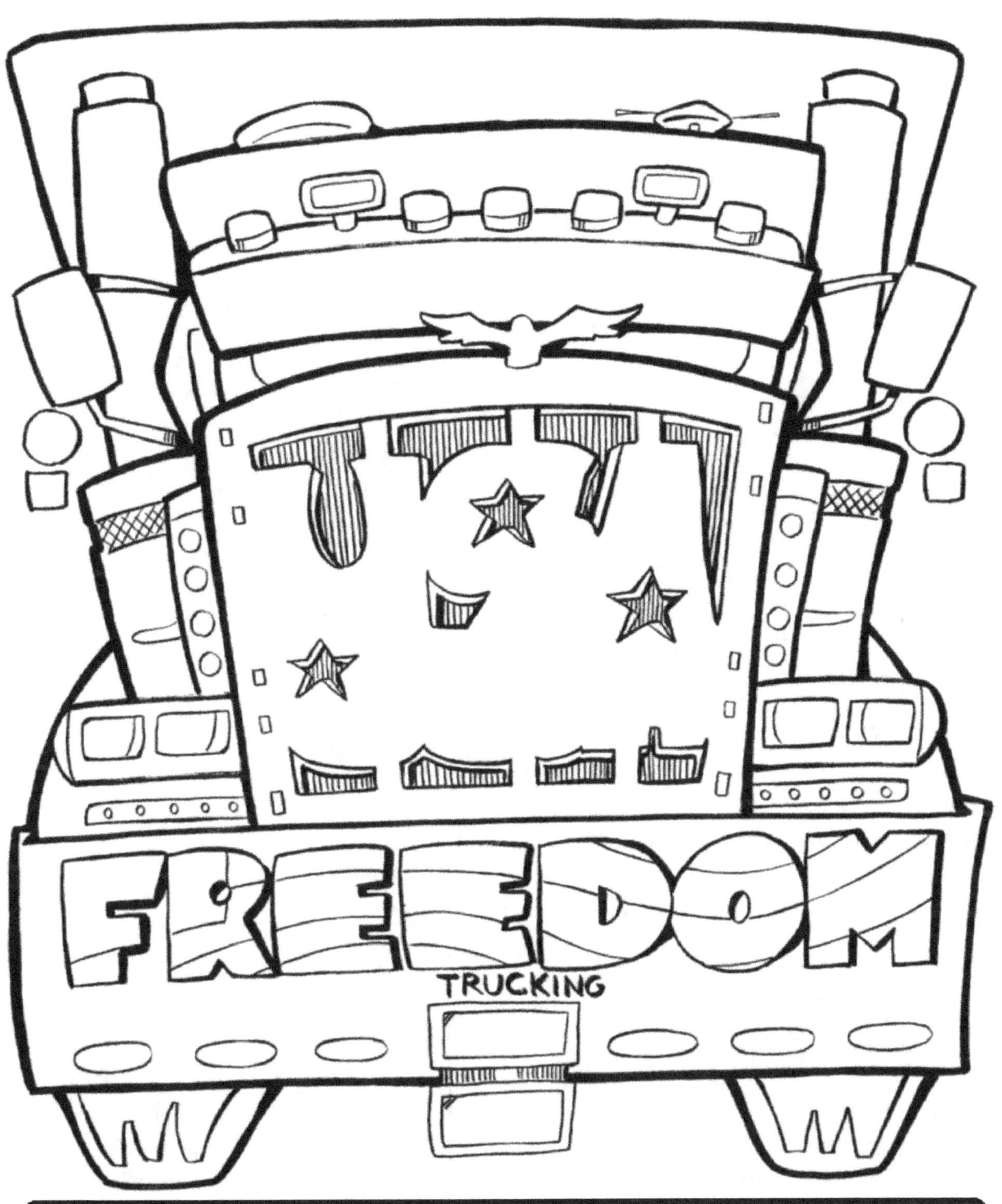

- A Kenworth 900 Was Named the "World's Most Custom" Truck in 2017
- A 'Beauty Contest' is held Every Year in Texas for Semi-Trucks! (That Makes for One Strange Swim-suit Competition!)

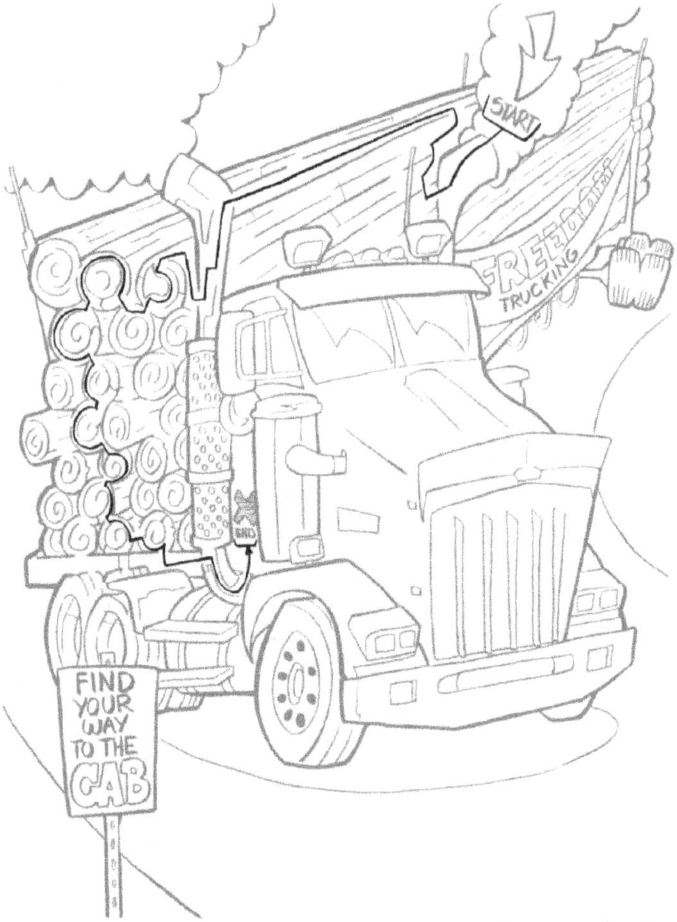

START
FREEDOM TRUCKING
END
FIND YOUR WAY TO THE CAB

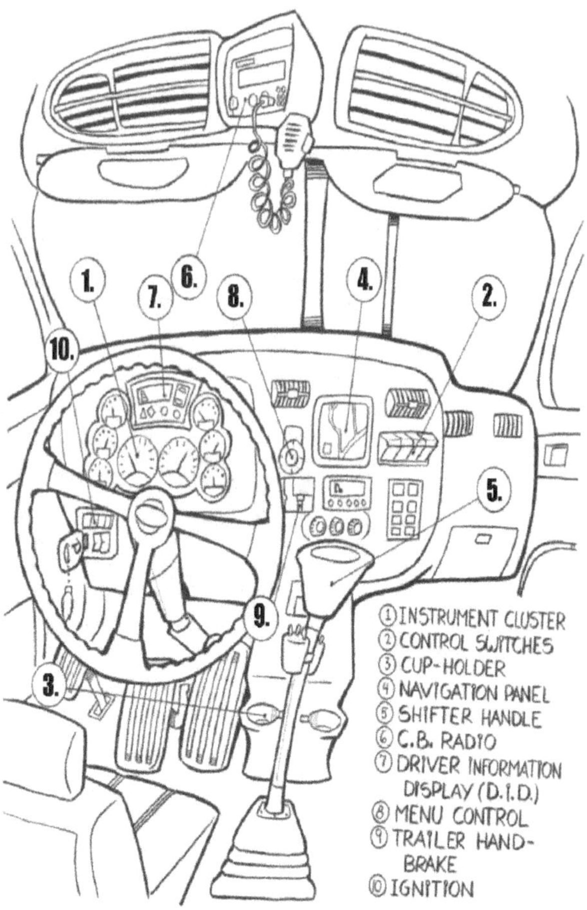

1. 2. 3. 4. 5. 6. 7. 8. 9. 10.

1. INSTRUMENT CLUSTER
2. CONTROL SWITCHES
3. CUP-HOLDER
4. NAVIGATION PANEL
5. SHIFTER HANDLE
6. C.B. RADIO
7. DRIVER INFORMATION DISPLAY (D.I.D.)
8. MENU CONTROL
9. TRAILER HAND-BRAKE
10. IGNITION

ANSWER PAGE

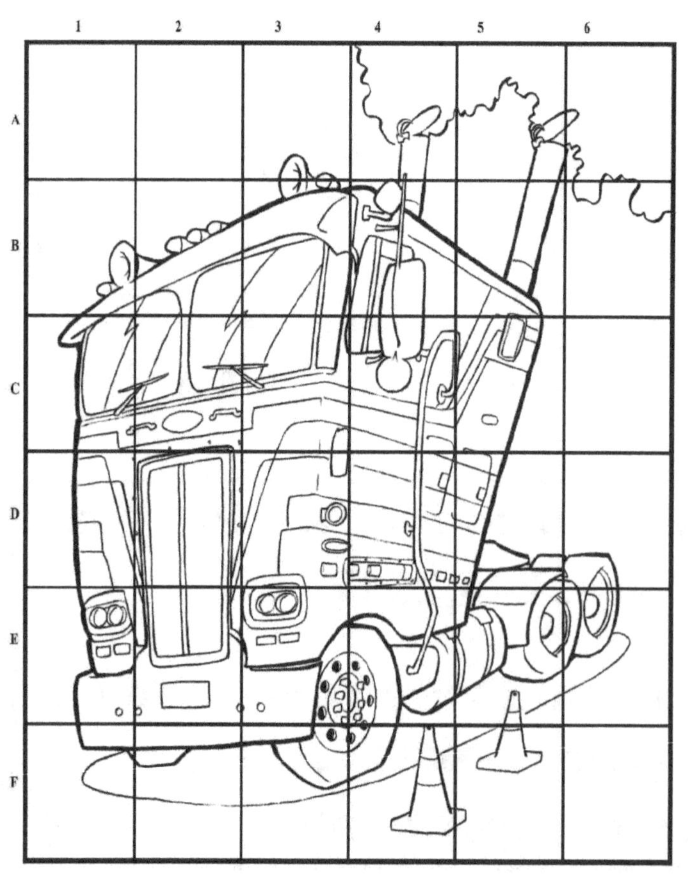

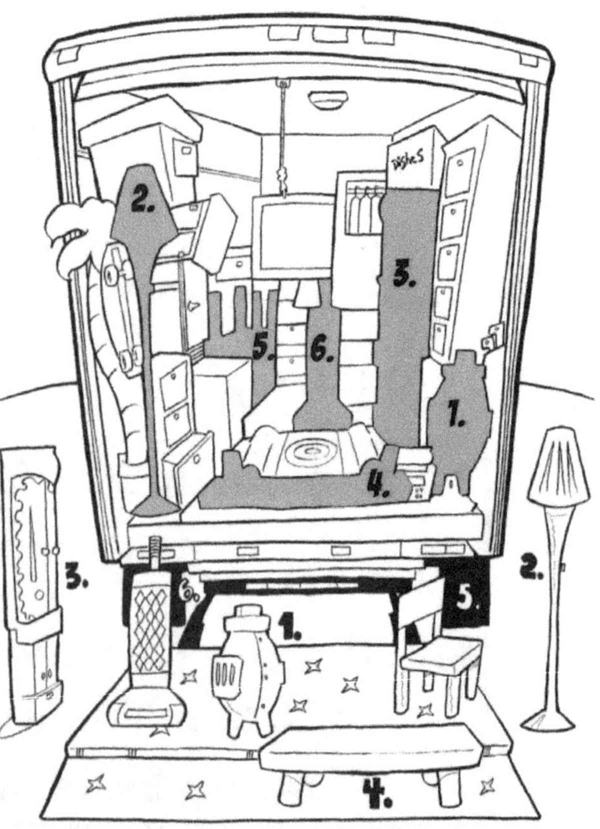

www.ingramcontent.com/pod-product-compliance
Lightning Source LLC
LaVergne TN
LVHW061258100826
845148LV00008B/1168

* 9 7 9 8 9 8 6 5 3 2 0 3 5 *